About Allison Bottke's
Setting Boundaries® books...

In 2008, author Allison Bottke launched her Setting Boundaries series of books with the publication of *Setting Boundaries with Your Adult Children*. That book has now sold more than 150,000 copies and has helped countless parents deal with the fallout of having adult children who have never taken responsibility for their own lives.

In the years since she wrote *Setting Boundaries with Your Adult Children*, Allison has added these important titles to her series:

Setting Boundaries with Your Aging Parents
Setting Boundaries with Difficult People
Setting Boundaries with Food
Setting Boundaries for Women

This new book, *A Young Woman's Guide to Setting Boundaries*, encourages teens to make smart choices and cope with stress by looking at the role boundaries play in life and love. As in the previous books in the Setting Boundaries series, Allison offers the valuable SANITY acronym to help you regain your sanity by setting appropriate boundaries and sticking to them.

Allison Bottke writes from the heart. She digs deep into her own experience with the complex issues people face daily. In Allison, you'll find a compassionate friend—and an author whose words can help you change your life.

For more information about the books in Allison's Setting Boundaries series, please turn to the back of this book.

A Young Woman's Guide to Setting Boundaries

Allison Bottke

HARVEST HOUSE PUBLISHERS
EUGENE, OREGON

Cover by Garborg Design Works, Savage, Minnesota

Published in association with the literary agency of The Steve Laube Agency, LLC, 5025 N. Central Ave., #635, Phoenix, Arizona, 85012.

SETTING BOUNDARIES is a registered trademark of The Hawkins Children's LLC. Harvest House Publishers, Inc. is the exclusive licensee of the federally registered trademark SETTING BOUNDARIES.

This book contains stories in which people's names and some details of their situations have been changed to protect their privacy.

A YOUNG WOMAN'S GUIDE TO SETTING BOUNDARIES

Copyright © 2014 by Allison Bottke
Published by Harvest House Publishers
Eugene, Oregon 97402
www.harvesthousepublishers.com

Library of Congress Cataloging-in-Publication Data
    Bottke, Allison.
    A young woman's guide to setting boundaries / Allison Bottke.
        pages cm
    Includes bibliographical references.
    ISBN 978-0-7369-5669-7 (pbk.)
    ISBN 978-0-7369-5670-3 (eBook)
    1. Teenage girls—Religious life. 2. Teenage girls—Conduct of life. 3. Christian teenagers—Religious life. 4. Christian teenagers—Conduct of life. 5. Interpersonal conflict—Religious aspects—Christianity. 6. Interpersonal relations—Religious aspects—Christianity. I. Title.
    BV4551.3.B68 2014
    248.8'33—dc23

                                                                    2013048204

Printed in the United States of America

                14 15 16 17 18 19 20 21 22 / VP-JH / 10 9 8 7 6 5 4 3 2 1

To Steve Laube
And to my Harvest House family
You have loved, supported, and encouraged me with
your words, actions, and truth.
You have taught me with your leadership, wisdom, and faith.
I am a better person for having known you.
I am deeply grateful.

May God continue to richly bless your lives
as you have blessed mine.

*Let the peace of Christ rule in your hearts, since as members
of one body you were called to peace. And be thankful. Let
the message of Christ dwell among you richly as you teach
and admonish one another with all wisdom through
psalms, hymns, and songs from the Spirit, singing to
God with gratitude in your hearts. And whatever you
do, whether in word or deed, do it all in the name of the
Lord Jesus, giving thanks to God the Father through him.*

Colossians 3:15-17

Contents

Foreword

by Tricia Goyer

I couldn't believe I was only 15 years old and having to make this decision. I was sitting in a Planned Parenthood office, and the woman across from me was discussing my pregnancy. She looked me in the eye and talked to me woman-to-woman.

"You're smart, and you have a good future ahead of you. I'd suggest you have an abortion," she said. "It's a simple procedure, and then you can continue with your life. You can finish high school and go to college. I know you won't regret it."

I listened to her and took her advice, but she couldn't have been more wrong. I did regret my abortion—not that I'd tell anyone that for many years. Instead, I tried to mask my pain by sleeping with guys, drinking with friends on the weekends, and with losing myself in soap operas or long novels that took my mind off real life.

My bad decisions started long before that day at Planned Parenthood. Starting in elementary school, I had crushes on my classmates, and I longed for love and attention. When an older guy finally gave that attention to me, I thought I'd fallen in love. I thought he was the one I'd be with forever. When he moved away, I was crushed, and I continued to date and to give myself to other guys, hoping to find fulfillment. I never found it. Not there. Not with him. Not with any high school boyfriend.

I'd grown up going to church, and I knew right from wrong. I knew not to listen to music with foul language, or watch horror shows, or sleep with my boyfriend, but no one ever taught me how to make wise decisions. No one ever taught me how to set boundaries...or even why they were important. So when I slipped up once, I just assumed I'd blown it and there was no hope for me. So why not slip up again? And again? I didn't understand that every day could be a new day to make positive changes.

The adults in my life didn't know how to help me. My mother never wanted to cause conflict between us, so she rarely said anything about my choices. Looking back I see now that she was more interested in being my friend than my parent. So instead of trying to find out why my choices weren't satisfying me, I kept trying to find happiness in all the wrong ways.

By the time I found myself pregnant again two years later, I was in a different frame of mind. I realized boundaries weren't meant to keep us from having fun. Boundaries were for protection, for guidance. I learned that my emotions didn't have to guide my decisions. Yes, my heart could want something, but that didn't mean it was best for me—it didn't mean I should pursue it. I also learned that I could turn unhealthy habits, impure thoughts, and unwholesome actions over to Jesus.

So I became a mom at age 17, and even though I haven't always made perfect choices, Jesus has walked beside me. When I didn't have the strength to stand firm, He gave me strength. Jesus showed me I didn't have to try to stick to my boundaries alone. He longed to be there for me. And what a difference it made when I turned to Him! He brought me an amazing husband and five more kids—three through adoption. Today, I write books, encourage other moms, and travel the world. It's ironic that I thought boundaries would keep me from having fun...instead they opened up my world in ways I never imagined!

For the past 12 years, I've led a support group for teenage mothers. Currently, I serve in inner-city Little Rock, and these young mothers come from generation after generation of men and women who didn't know how to set healthy boundaries and who continue to make wrong, hurtful choices.

As I've worked weekly with these young women, I've seen them face the same struggles I once faced. But I've seen some of them learn to set healthy boundaries in their lives. As a result, I've seen their lives transform, benefiting not only themselves but also their children! I've also seen them reach out to other young women, encouraging them that they, too, can set boundaries before they make too many wrong choices. They're helping others in ways no one ever helped them! And that's the whole point. Our positive choices can influence others. When you place healthy boundaries in your life, you not only reap the benefits, but others do too.

And that's why I love *A Young Women's Guide to Setting Boundaries*. Allison shares her story, and she offers help, advice, and encouragement through these pages. I wish I had this advice when I was younger! It's impossible to go back and rewind time, but it *is* possible to help others along the way. I am so thankful for this resource. I'm excited about using it with the young women I mentor. I'm also excited that the advice in these pages will help *you*.

You are making a wonderful choice today by picking up this book. In these pages you'll discover habits that will help you become a better person. Many adults don't understand the importance of setting healthy boundaries. Instead they find themselves in one vicious cycle after another—running on the gerbil wheel of insanity Allison talks about. As you grasp these principles and learn to apply the SANITY Steps, you will be ahead of the game.

When you set boundaries, you are holding off what seems good at the moment, and you're saving your mind, heart, emotions, and will for what is best for life. No one can live a perfect life without mistakes, yet today you can make choices to bring positive changes to your life—and it all starts with believing you are worth God's best.

Cheering for you!

Tricia Goyer

Introduction

Life is filled with choices, and learning how to make *smart* choices by setting healthy boundaries can change the entire story of your life.

When I was a teen, all I cared about was pushing boundaries, expanding boundaries, and fighting against boundaries. Frankly, I didn't see a whole lot of value in setting boundaries at all.

Big mistake. *Huge.*

I've often wondered if things would have been different in my life if I had known someone courageous enough to get up in my face and explain the concept of boundaries to me and help me implement some corrective boundaries to protect me from a lot of unnecessary pain. Even after many of my boundaries were violated, if I had known the power that was available to me if I established new healthy boundaries, the entire course of my life would have been changed. I wish someone had told me how I could effectively deal with the pain and confusion in my life and with the overwhelming stress that often accompanied my chaotic emotions.

> I wish someone had told me how I could effectively deal with the pain and confusion in my life and with the overwhelming stress that often accompanied my chaotic emotions.

Though the world today is quite different than it was when I was your age, I can promise you that the pain and emptiness I felt back then is no different from what you may feel today. And the longing to love and be loved is no different today than it was when I ran away from home in Cleveland, Ohio, to New York City when I was 14.

I was lost, afraid, and looking for love, security, and happiness. I longed for someone who would understand and validate who I really was—and who wouldn't try to make me into someone I wasn't.

Never one to follow trends, I had always marched to the beat of my own drum. I didn't have a lot of friends in school. I had a low tolerance for boredom and frequently questioned the rules, especially when they didn't seem to fit the situation. Back then, adults often called me impulsive, distracted, and rebellious—a dreamer who needed to stop living in fantasyland. In reality, I was driven by imagination, creativity, and a passion for discovery that made it naturally easy for me to take risks—but incredibly difficult to fit into a structured classroom environment. My intuition and sensitivity gave me a heightened awareness of things—something that I noticed other kids around me didn't seem to have. Truthfully, my brain fired on multiple channels, and most teachers were intent on getting students to focus on one channel at a time. I couldn't do that if my life depended on it.

Today, those of us who have ADD (attention deficit disorder) may be neurologically poised to adapt more quickly to an ever-changing environment. However, when I was growing up, all of my differences (which included dyslexia) made me feel like a misfit—a freak. I didn't know how to fit in. And when you're a teenager, it's very important to fit in, to feel special. I suspect you know what I mean even if your issues are somewhat different from mine.

Jerry was the one who first made me feel special. I was 14 when I met him at our local Dairy Queen one summer afternoon. He was an 18-year-old guy from out of town who immediately took an interest in me. In almost no time, I fell head over heels in love. I knew I had met my Prince Charming—the man who would love and care for me the rest of my life.

Unfortunately, my mother didn't agree. She didn't like Jerry, so I began to sneak out of the house to see him. This was the first of what would become a long list of big mistakes.

Even though I was only 14, I was old for my age. A creative, tenacious, and strong-willed child raised by a single working mother, I had grown up fast. I was also very developed, and at five feet seven, people thought I was years older than I was. And so when my mother threatened to send me away if I continued to see Jerry, I took matters into my own hands and ran away from home. Actually, it was Jerry's idea, and at the time I was too blinded by love to think for myself. I would have done anything he told me to do.

"There's no way she's going to keep us apart," Jerry said as he handed me the money for my airplane ticket and $200 to tide me over until I found a job. "I made a reservation for you to leave tomorrow. Pack a bag and get out before she gets home. This will show your mother how serious we are. Here's the phone number of my friends in New York—they'll put you up for a while. Call them as soon as you land."

Jerry was my first love, and the thought of my mother forbidding me to see him was unbearable. Even though I was only 14 and had never even been on a plane, the thought of traveling to New York City and living with strangers didn't bother me. I never stopped long enough to consider the possible consequences of this choice.

On the Streets of New York

Landing at LaGuardia Airport in New York on a Saturday evening, I began a journey that would change my life. Hurrying to a pay phone to call Jerry's friends, I thought about this luxurious, newfound freedom. I would find a job, and in a few weeks, Jerry would join me. We'd get married and live happily ever after. I was so clueless. As the phone rang, I dreamed of married life, of the idyllic way everything would turn out.

"The number you have reached is no longer in service…" I jumped at the sound of the recording. *I must have dialed wrong*, I thought. Trying again, this time more carefully, I began to feel apprehension creep through my body.

"The number you have reached is no longer…" It was true. The number was disconnected. I hung up the phone and stood still.

I couldn't reach Jerry—he had rented a room without a phone. (This was long before cell phones were commonplace.)

Okay, I said to myself, *this isn't the end of the world. Find a hotel or a YWCA until you can reach Jerry at work in the morning.* I'm not sure how or what I knew about the YWCA at that age, only that I could find shelter there.

I forced myself to look on the bright side. I was in New York City—the Big Apple! Being a creative person, my first thought was of Greenwich Village—a city that was always in the news and known for welcoming creative people. Surely in the Village I could find a place to stay the night. It mattered little to me that it was starting to get late and that I reeked of "vulnerable underage runaway."

I took the subway from the airport, not frightened in the least. I grew up poor in Cleveland, and we always took public transportation. The subway felt a lot like the Regional Transit Authority system I knew.

When I finally arrived at my destination, the Village was aglow in lights, a street festival was underway, and artists lined the corridor. Singers, street dancers, and vendors were everywhere, just like on television. I had paid for a taxi in Cleveland, snacks at both airports, and phone calls and the subway in New York, but I still had about $150—a lot of money, or so I thought. In reality, I didn't have a clue about what it would cost to live on my own for a day, let alone a week, a month, or more. When I stopped at a hotel in the Village, they told me it was $50 for the night. "Seriously?" I gasped. Were hotels really that expensive? At that rate, I'd be out of money in three days, with nothing extra for food or transportation.

Fear began to grip my heart, but I fought it with all my might.

By 11:00 that night, the street vendors were beginning to close up shop. Artists were packing up, and the warm hum of people hustling and bustling was being replaced by another kind of atmosphere. Women in very short dresses appeared. Men with lots of jewelry and fancy cars lined the streets. People passed each other bottles and strange-smelling cigarettes. I held tightly to my suitcase and continued to walk, repeating to myself that everything would be fine.

Then I saw her artwork—canvas seemingly touched by God. Paintings and pencil sketch drawings hung on the fence, their content calling out to me. Mom had often taken my siblings and me to the art museum, and I appreciated many forms of art. My heart raced.

"Can I help you?" I looked up to the round, pleasant face of an older woman.

"Did you draw these?" I asked in awe. "I love them! Oh, I'd love to have talent like that!"

"Everyone has some special talent, my dear. I'm sure you'll find yours one day," she said. "My name is Tanya. What's yours?"

I can't recall what we talked about next, but eventually I asked if she knew where I might find a YWCA. At that question, she looked me straight in the eye and without hesitation said, "Please, come home for the evening with my daughter, Claudette, and me. We have plenty of room. This city is a difficult place to get around in during the daytime and even worse at night. You can get a room tomorrow."

Concerned by the lack of easy alternatives, I accepted her offer. Today, I shudder to think what may have happened to me if I had said no or if she hadn't turned out to be such a wonderful person. Back then, I didn't know that predators sometimes masqueraded as kind and caring helpers. The same is even truer today, and vulnerable teenage girls continue to be forced into prostitution, drug addiction, and sex trafficking. Chances today are slim that a runaway teen alone on the streets of a big city will randomly connect with an honest and caring person who is willing to open her home and her heart. I have no doubt that had I remained on the dangerous streets of New York City, I would have become another runaway statistic. The Bible says, "No evil will conquer you; no plague will come near your home. For he will order his angels to protect you wherever you go" (Psalm 91:10-11 NLT). That night, the Lord sent my angel. Her name was Tanya Cervone.

Abandoned and Afraid

The next morning I called the warehouse where Jerry worked, only to find out he had been fired the previous week. Calling my best friend in Cleveland, I then learned the police were looking for me. My fairy tale had quickly turned into a nightmare. My world was falling apart, but I was determined to hang on, determined no one would know how frightened I was.

After that series of unsettling early morning phone calls, I found a YWCA in the phone book. I planned to leave Tanya's apartment, get myself a room at the Y, and hit the streets to find a job. I couldn't waste even one day.

Other than occasional babysitting, I had never had a job. Having watched Macy's Thanksgiving Day parade every year, I thought I'd start at Macy's and apply for a job as a salesclerk. I was courageous but clueless as I put on the only dress I brought, thanked Tanya for her hospitality, and asked her for directions. I thought I had fooled Tanya, but I hadn't—not for a minute. She had listened in on my frantic phone calls.

"I have an idea," she said. "Please stay here with us until you find a job. I'm sure you'll find something in no time, and then you can get yourself a little apartment. Those rooms at the Y are so small and dingy."

I had to admit, Tanya's apartment would definitely be more comfortable, and I would be able to save some money, so I accepted. However, with false bravado, I made it very clear that I intended to get a job. She did not try to dissuade me.

That afternoon, in the subway on my way to Macy's, I felt certain everything would be okay, even though a sick feeling was roiling in the pit of my stomach.

Years later I learned that while I was gone that first day, Tanya went through my things, located my mom's name and phone number, and contacted her in Ohio. Tanya assured Mom that I was okay. She said the police might be able to get me home, but they wouldn't be able to keep me there. "She has to go home on her own. Otherwise, she'll only run again," Tanya told my mom. "Trust me—I think maybe I can reach her."

During the next few days, I was repeatedly turned down for jobs because I didn't have acceptable identification or any work history. I grew more and more confused and frightened. I finally reached Jerry, but I was hardly comforted when he called me a crybaby and said if I really loved him, I'd "get it together and get enough money" to help him come out to join me since he had given me all of his available cash.

"Do whatever you have to do," he hissed at me over the phone. "You're in New York City. Figure something out soon. I've gotta get out of here, and you owe me." With that, he hung up on me.

That should have been another clue that he wasn't concerned about my best interests or even my safety. The first clue should have been that he would send me to New York City without being absolutely certain I would have a place to stay.

Unable to stand the fear any longer, I tearfully confided in Tanya. She asked me serious, personal questions, and she listened carefully to my responses. It was as though a dam had burst. We talked for hours.

She shared her wisdom, gave me thoughtful advice, and validated my feelings. She spoke of what it was like to be an artist, what it was like to create paintings from her mind's eye. She talked of her life in another country and her own challenges, and she encouraged me to talk about mine. Never before had I shared such intimate feelings with an adult and been so totally accepted.

My mother and I had never discussed personal things. I didn't know that kind of communication existed. Tanya helped me to think rationally and not emotionally, and a few days later I decided to go home. I only wish I had been able to continue that level of communication with someone when I returned home. If I had, things may have turned out differently.

> She reached out and protected a vulnerable, frightened teenager who was pretending to have it all together.

I never saw Tanya again, yet our Christmas cards and letters were as consistent as the seasons until she passed away a few years ago. When I learned of her death, I stood in the post office and cried, and then I smiled at my memory of her. She reached out and protected a vulnerable, frightened teenager who was pretending to have it all together. She exhibited the unconditional love of Christ in the truest and purest way. In all probability, she saved my life.

Tanya truly wanted what was best for me, but she also knew that I had to be the one to make the decision to return home. I had to accept responsibility for my choices and the consequences of my actions.

Are You Ready?

Because you're reading this book, I believe you're ready to make some important decisions. Maybe the adults in your life don't quite understand what you're going through. Maybe you don't understand it yourself. Perhaps the pressure around you is overwhelming and you realize something needs to change, but you aren't quite sure what that something is.

If that's the case, I'd like to introduce you to the power of boundaries.

This secret is too seldom practiced, but it can transform your life. It can help you cope with your stress and empower you to make smart choices on your journey to become the woman God wants you to be.

I won't lie to you—I've made some monumentally poor choices in my life. And the truth is, I'm still learning how to become the woman God wants me to be. I surely don't know it all. In fact, I'm not a highly educated woman, if you base education on the number of years spent in formal classrooms.

> The choices you make today will determine the quality of your life—not only tomorrow but also for years to come.

However, I'm quite familiar with the pressure of teenage stress. I know what it's like to be different and yet want desperately to fit in. I know what it's like when your emotions are raw, your heart aches, and you think no one can possibly understand. And I know the choices you make today will determine the quality of your life—not only tomorrow but also for years to come. And I believe you care about the quality of your life—otherwise, you wouldn't be reading a book on how to make smart choices.

When I was your age, I didn't fully grasp how my choices would affect the quality of my life, and I quickly got off track—and I mean *seriously* off track. When I returned home from New York, nothing had really changed in my situation or in my thought process, and I continued to make increasingly poor choices. When I turned 15, I made a disastrous choice to run away again, this time to get married—a choice that had far more devastating and life-threatening consequences. It set off a chain reaction of events that changed the course of my life—and ultimately the life of another person who was not yet born.

The Lessons We Learn

Perhaps you've heard the expression "One bad apple spoils the whole bunch."

Bad choices can be that way—they can infect whatever they touch. And they have a tendency to lead to additional bad choices that can spoil everything around us if they aren't plucked from the basket of life and addressed properly so they are not repeated.

When we handle our mistakes rightly, they can be some of our greatest teachers. The tragedy comes when we don't learn the lesson and end up repeating the same mistakes over and over again.

The choices I made as a teenager changed the course of my adult life. Unfortunately, many of those choices were not very smart, and I never seemed to learn from my mistakes. My feelings of unworthiness and my lack of identity often motivated me in unhealthy and stress-filled ways, and I continued on a self-destructive path for many years.

That's why I'm so passionate about this topic today.

I know I can't go back. And I know God has a plan for the journey I've taken. Even so, I have far too many regrets from poor choices, and my prayer is that you will have much fewer.

The Hole in My Heart

As a teen, I looked confident and optimistic on the outside. But on the inside, I had almost no sense of personal identity or self-worth, and unfortunately that fueled many of my poor choices. A lot of painful things had happened to me as a little girl. And in school, I found out I had a learning disability (dyslexia). Later, I was also diagnosed with ADD. Because of these things, I often felt lost, afraid, and horribly alone. I didn't feel as if anyone understood or I had anyone to talk to, least of all my mother. I didn't appreciate my value as a person. I also didn't understand that my lack of boundaries and my frantic teenage search for love, understanding, and purpose would end up in pain, not happiness. I didn't understand that I could actually set healthy boundaries for myself as a teen—or that I was even worthy of doing so. I *did* have that power, but I didn't realize it. You have that power too, but you might not realize it either.

Truthfully, setting healthy limits and managing conflicting emotions is a never-ending process for women, no matter how old we are. However, the quest for meaning and love can be especially challenging for teens, who are still developing in many ways. You're trying on different personas in a search for your identity. The hormonal changes of puberty (what a yucky word, but there's really nothing else to explain this equally yucky time) are followed by the turbulence of adolescence. It's easy to become confused, frustrated, and simply lost. No wonder we sometimes make not-so-smart choices or passively go where we really don't want to go.

The weight of bad choices adds up quickly. The more baggage you accumulate throughout the years, the harder it becomes to unpack. If you're not careful, your mind and heart can begin to look like the inside of a house on a TV episode of *Hoarders*—desperately cluttered and dangerous to navigate. The only way to keep from getting buried under a mess of emotions and experiences is to learn two critical skills—setting healthy boundaries in your life, and making smart choices based on rational thinking and not just on emotional feelings.

As a teenager, you are perfectly capable of making good decisions when your mind is calm. But the part of your brain that helps you manage emotions is still developing, so for a while, you'll naturally have a harder time calming your emotions down. When that happens, bad judgment often overrides good judgment.

Have you ever done or said something you regretted once you took time to really think about it?

It's good to have emotions, to be able to feel things deeply and passionately. However, trouble comes when we lack self-control and place our feelings and emotions above our safety or above someone else's safety.

That's what happened when I was 14 and ran away from home and flew to New York City. It happened when I was 15 and got married. It happened when I was 16 and I thought the incredible love I felt for my unborn child qualified me to be a mother.

What was I thinking?

The fact is, I wasn't *thinking*; I was primarily *feeling*. I didn't stop long enough to think through the possible consequences of any of my actions. Let's be totally honest. How often do you stop to see if your brain is in agreement with the emotions your heart is generating? Have you ever done or said something you regretted once you took time to really think about it? If so, you understand how emotions can easily get the upper hand.

Stopping to think carefully and critically when you're feeling emotional isn't something that comes naturally for most teenagers. And when adults are being honest, it's often difficult for many of us as well. However, it's a skill you can learn, a healthy habit you can develop. And developing this vital skill as a teen can change your life.

Change Starts When We Stop

The question is, do you want to develop a habit that can make you a better person, a happier person, a more loving person? A person whom others treat with respect? Do you want to learn a skill that will help you cope with the increasing stress you're feeling? A skill that will enable you to have more control of your own life?

Right now, you may feel that you have no real control of your life. That may be true in some aspects, but it's certainly not true in all of them.

The fact is, you *can* control how you think, and you *can* learn to think in ways that will improve your attitude and your actions—in ways that will help you feel better about yourself and will help peers and adults take you more seriously. You *can* control how you respond to people and situations. You *can* learn how to live within limits that will empower you— in ways that will give you less baggage to carry into adulthood and ultimately provide you with more freedom and less stress than you ever imagined.

> God has given you the ability to think for yourself and to control your attitude and behavior.

God has given you the ability to think for yourself and to control your attitude and behavior. However, your ability to exercise this control in healthy ways is still developing, and you are no doubt still discovering God's plan and purpose for your life. That's why it's important to know your tremendous worth and value to God as you make decisions now that will change your future.

It's no accident you're reading this book. Whether you bought it for yourself or someone gave it to you, God is calling you to be courageous and faithful.

Are you willing to take up the challenge?

I know it's tough to see good in anything when the pressure of stress is closing in around you. That's why I'd like to introduce you to boundaries—and to SANITY.

The Skill of SANITY

Learning the Six Steps to SANITY and using them as decision-making tools to set and maintain healthy boundaries will bring you hope and direction in any challenging situation or relationship throughout your life—not just during these stressful teen years.

I know you've got a lot on your mind and on your plate, but I hope you'll let me introduce you to a perspective on life that will transform how you think and quite possibly rock your world.

You may feel that many of the adults around you just don't get it. They don't get how hard it is to be a teenage girl. However, many of us *do* get it—we're just not always sure how to convey that to you, our precious daughters, granddaughters, nieces, and loved ones.

I was brutally abused and molested as a toddler. I suffered from undiagnosed learning disabilities growing up. I ran away from home as a teen, quit school, and married my boyfriend, who beat me, raped me, and almost killed me. I got divorced, became a mother, got my GED, had an abortion, gained 100 pounds, discovered diet pills, attended cosmetology school, and subsequently gave up on myself, on love, and on God—all before I turned 18.

Trust me, I'm not your typical advice-offering adult.

I totally get how hard it is to be a teenage girl, and I hope you'll give me a chance to share some of the secrets I've learned along the way. Secrets that can help you deal with your pain and problems. Secrets that can open doors to unimaginable joy, success, and love.

1

The Truth About Smart Choices

The mirror of our culture tells us that self-worth comes from good looks, popularity, and money. The truth is, self-worth comes from character, competence, and smart choices.

By the time you're a teen, your life has already been influenced by many people and events, mostly out of your control. So here are three important questions:

1. Do you believe you can choose who and what will influence you?
2. Whom and what will you allow to influence your future?
3. Will you accept responsibility for the consequences of your choices?

Being a teenager has always been difficult, but you're likely to be facing greater challenges than people did in previous generations. You have more to worry about than puberty and adolescence—which are challenging enough—or what you're going to do after high school graduation. The issues today are far more life-changing or even life-threatening. Look closely at the following list of things kids are stressing over today.

alcohol abuse

abuse of prescription and
illegal drugs

anxiety and stress

body image and appearance

the choking game

college decisions

cyberbullying

dating violence

depression

eating disorders

gang violence

Internet predators

mental health problems

obesity

parents' addictions

peer pressure

performance and measuring up

poverty

school pressure

sex trafficking

sexual pressure

social media struggles

suicide

teen pregnancy

youth violence

Statistics indicate that you are likely to be dealing with one or more of these tough topics. If that's the case, please hang in there, help is on the way! Never underestimate God's ability to bring you exactly what you need just when you need it the most, whether it's a book, movie, person, thought, idea, or even a powerful self-realization—an epiphany. "Epiphany"—isn't that a great word?

> Never underestimate God's ability to bring you exactly what you need just when you need it the most...

The Choice of Vocabulary

My mom loved crossword puzzles, and when I was growing up, we owned more dictionaries than Bibles. Mom didn't finish high school, but she had an excellent command of the English language, and I have distinct memories of her challenging me to learn new words. We often played a game in which I would open the dictionary at random and point to a word. Sometimes I knew the word, but most often I didn't. The goal was to use that word correctly whenever possible throughout the day. I don't recall winning anything other than Mom's admiration, but that was always enough.

However, I now see that I was winning so much more.

Thanks to my mother's influence, I appreciated words and understood their meanings from a very early age. It always drove me crazy when adults assumed I was too young to understand complex words or they were surprised when I used one correctly. I distinctly remember how much I hated that, especially as a teenager. Perhaps I was just overly sensitive, but I don't think so.

So I want you to know I'm not going to dumb down my words and use only those I think you might understand. Instead, I encourage you to use a dictionary if you don't fully grasp a particular word I use. Learning new words will open doors to a broader understanding of your world.

"Epiphany" was one of the words I learned playing that dictionary game with my mom. I loved the way it sounded, but I also loved its meaning. An epiphany is an experience of sudden and striking realization. Webster defines it as a moment in which you suddenly see or understand something in a new or very clear way. We most often hear the word used to describe a scientific breakthrough or a religious or philosophical discovery. You can have an epiphany too—whenever an enlightening realization allows you to understand a problem or situation from a new and deeper perspective.

My prayer is that you will come to personally embrace this word. In fact, one of my goals with this book is for you to have an epiphany about your power to determine your future—for good or for bad.

The Choice of Intentional Change

Learning new words, making new choices, and experiencing an epiphany reminds me of one of my favorite movies. If you haven't seen it, I encourage you to stream it online or rent the DVD.

If you Google *Born Yesterday*, you'll find there are two versions of this movie. I first saw the 1950 version when I was a kid. I loved watching classic black-and-white films on television, and this one was great. The 1993 remake is even better, and this is the one I encourage you to see. Billie

Dawn (Melanie Griffith) is an ex-showgirl, Harry Brock (John Goodman) is her corrupt millionaire boyfriend, and Paul Verrall (Don Johnson) is her brainy tutor.

Harry takes Billie with him to Washington (where he tries to buy off a congressman). He becomes disgusted with Billie's ignorance and lack of manners (though he himself is much worse), and he hires Paul to educate his bimbo-like girlfriend and teach her how to appear more intelligent. Blossoming under Paul's encouragement, Billie turns out to be much smarter than anybody knew and begins to think for herself. In the process, she learns just how corrupt her boyfriend is. Things become more complicated as she begins questioning the papers Harry keeps telling her to sign and as Paul begins to fall in love with her.

The 1993 remake includes a great library scene. Billie is reading a book Paul has given her, and she keeps getting up to consult a big dictionary that sits at the front of the room on a lectern. Eventually, Paul buys her a pocket dictionary she can keep with her.

Both versions of the film contain thought-provoking references about character, integrity, competence, change, and choice. Billie experiences one epiphany after another as she realizes that her corrupt boyfriend is using her, that she isn't a dumb blonde after all, and that it's up to her to make different choices. Billie Dawn is a woman who makes many intentional choices to change her life.

Her process of change is sometimes painful, especially when Harry gets violent, but Billie refuses to remain the same. She learns what doesn't matter—what happened in the past or where she came from. She also learns what does matter—the future and where she is going. And so she stops ignoring her pain and problems, she pushes herself beyond constricting boundaries, she courageously addresses violated boundaries, and she boldly establishes new boundaries.

As a result, Billie discovers her self-worth and the power she has to direct and change the course of her life.

My prayer is that you will learn the same during our time together.

Where You Come from Doesn't Matter

Regardless of where you come from, regardless of your situations or circumstances, you share a common bond with every teenage girl today.

You live in a world of infinite possibilities and sometimes frightening realities.

You may come from privilege or from poverty. You might receive everything you want or have to fight for everything you have. You may have incredibly kind and loving parents or not so much—perhaps even the total opposite. You may have grown up with your own bedroom or have shared a room with siblings, cousins, aunts, or even grandma. You may live in an area where multiple generations of your family have lived, or you may have no idea what it's like to call any place home because you've been uprooted so often. You may have plans to go to college, or you might just be trying to make it through today.

You might know what it feels like to have a loving father—a positive male role model who is actively involved in your life. Yet the truth is, many teen girls have never heard an encouraging word or declaration of love from their father. Others have never met their father, and some don't even know who their biological dad is.

Those are things you have not been able to control. But as you move into adulthood, you'll find that what happened in your past doesn't have to dictate your future. You always have choices. You can let the past remain in the past, and you can choose a happier future.

> Although many things will influence you along the pathway of life, you are ultimately who you are because of your own choices.

Your Choices Can Change the Story of Your Life

Although many things will influence you along the pathway of life, you are ultimately who you are because of your own choices. This is sometimes hard to admit, especially if someone has hurt, controlled, or enabled you. In these cases, you could easily blame someone else for your lot in life. In fact, you can become so accustomed to blaming others for your situations and circumstances that it's difficult to see the part you play in the drama of your own life. You might blame peer pressure, your boyfriend, society, parents, teachers, or adults in general. Maybe you even blame God. On occasion, maybe you even blame yourself. You may think you're not good enough, smart enough, pretty enough, thin enough, and so on.

The truth is, you may have made your own bad decisions in the past, and now you're suffering the consequences and sometimes the guilt that follow bad decisions. But however you play the blame game, it isn't going to help you move on. It isn't going to empower you to be all that you can be.

You may have been an innocent victim. Things may have happened to you that were never your choice. *But that was then and this is now.* Now it's time to write a new chapter in your book of life. Now it's time to take responsibility for your choices and changes.

It's time to stop being a guest at your own pity party.

Where Choice Begins

You weren't born with the weight of stress you now carry. Boundaries are built—not inherited. A great deal about how you make choices today depends on what you learned as a child.

The fact is, you learned how to make choices as you watched the adults around you make their own choices. You also learned as others responded and reacted to the choices you were making, and you learned about accepting responsibility or rejecting accountability for the consequences of your choices.

Chances are, the first boundary you ever learned was the verbal cue of "no," and it was most likely accompanied by a raised voice and with feelings of pain, anger, or fear—your own, or that of someone close to you.

"No! Don't touch that!"

"No! Don't put that in your mouth!"

"No! Don't cry!"

We learn the meaning of *no* very early, and we begin to believe that most of the things associated with it are bad. Unfortunately, that initial negative aspect of boundaries can seep into our psyche and imprint itself on our mind, heart, and soul like a bad tattoo.

However, not all boundaries restrict bad behavior or potentially harmful situations. In fact, healthy boundaries can prevent problems in lots of areas. When we learn and embrace the incredible positive value of setting boundaries, we latch on to a powerful truth that can unlock doors and bring epiphany moments.

For example, let's say we see a mother shopping in the grocery store with her preschool daughter. Every aisle brings new and delightful attractions for the girl as her little hands reach and she tries to maneuver her body out of the shopping cart seat.

"Mommy, can I have this?"

"Mommy, I want that!"

"*Mommy!*"

This is a great boundary-teaching opportunity for parents, yet they often confuse their children and enable them to become master manipulators.

Young children don't understand they can't have everything they want—that something isn't good for them, is too expensive, or isn't age appropriate. All they understand is that something has caught their eye and that they want to hold it, play with it, or eat it. It's called instant gratification.

It's natural for young children to want the things they want. What isn't natural is for parents to allow young children to have everything they want. Sometimes, parents must say no, and how they say it makes all the difference in the world.

The most effective parents say no with firmness *and* love. They are consistent with their responses as their young children learn how to communicate, make choices, and accept consequences. They are patient as their young children discover how the world around them works.

Alas, this doesn't always happen.

As a young mother, I considered myself a firm disciplinarian, and when I said no I meant it—until I didn't. Which usually happened when I began to second-guess my response, feel guilty, or find myself in an emotional meltdown because of my own messed-up life. Then, I would give in to my son and do my best to provide whatever he wanted. I was trying to make myself feel better.

My son learned that my no was often inconsistent and usually based on emotional feeling rather than rational thinking. He learned that my no didn't always mean no.

My dysfunctional, codependent enabling habits started early. In retrospect, I can now see clearly how confusing my mixed messages must have been to my son. How could he learn about healthy boundaries from a mother who didn't understand them herself?

When you were a child, the adults around you may have understood the concept of healthy boundaries. They might have set consistent and healthy limits with firmness and love while encouraging you to develop your individuality. If this is the case, you are incredibly blessed.

However, if you received mixed messages about yes and no as a child, and especially if the primary adults around you were struggling with their own boundary issues (as I was), you may have developed some unhealthy habits that are now causing challenges in your life as a teen—habits you might not be completely aware of.

Write It Down

I don't remember a time when I didn't use writing as my primary method of communication. In fact, I have a humiliating memory of writing one of my very first declarations of undying love to a boy named Kenny when I was nine. He promptly attached my letter to the playground fence for all the neighborhood kids to read. At first I was horrified.

Then, as more and more kids stopped at the fence to read my words and pay attention to my feelings, I began to understand the power of the pen. Writing gave wings to my voice.

And so, before we go any further, I'd like to ask that you have a notebook or journal nearby while you're reading this book. I'll occasionally suggest that you jot something down or candidly answer some questions. Don't worry about spelling or story structure or about form or function. This isn't an English class assignment. This notebook is a private place for you to record your own thoughts and your candid responses to my questions. No one will see what you write unless you want them to.

And just for the record, letting others see what you're writing isn't necessarily a bad idea—especially if that someone is in a position to offer you wise advice and guidance. In which case, you may find it easier to articulate what you're thinking and feeling in writing. This can be a great way to open the lines of communication with someone if you so desire.

But there is a caveat to this writing exercise. Always be aware that what you disclose in writing might be seen, especially if there is a chance that someone in your home may not respect your privacy. And if an adult in your life has reason to believe you may be in danger, all privacy rules are void, and he or she has the right and even the responsibility to check your notebook.

All that said, open your journal now and write about the stress in your life. How would you like it to change? How might it be related to weak or nonexistent boundaries? Can you recall when and what you learned about boundaries as a little girl—good, bad, or indifferent? What did you learn about the consequences of choices? Think back to your earliest memories of learning the meaning of no. Stop for a moment and give this some thought.

Being able to *stop*, *step back*, and *think* is a critical aspect in your ability to make smart choices. In fact, the first step in finding sanity is to stop. We'll talk more about this step in a little while, but for now, just get yourself a notebook and write whatever comes to mind about boundaries.

2

The Scoop on Boundaries

Many people wrongly assume that boundaries always confine or limit us. But in reality, healthy boundaries do just the opposite. They free us to do things in life that really matter. They show us more clearly where not to waste our energies.

Two basic boundary categories define the way we interact with others and allow them to interact with us.

- physical boundaries
- psychological boundaries

> Without boundaries, our lives would be chaotic and filled with stress.

Without these boundaries, others could touch us in any way they wanted, do whatever they wished with our possessions, and treat us in any way they desired. In addition, we would believe everyone else's bad behaviors are our fault, take on everyone else's problems as our own, and feel as if we have no rights of our own. In short, without boundaries, our lives would be chaotic and filled with stress.

Maybe that describes your life now. If so, it need not describe your life in the future.

As a child, you depended on adults to fix all of your "boo-boos." You still depend in many ways on the adults in your life, but your independence is increasing, and it's important for you to be able to make smart choices about protecting your physical and psychological boundaries. To be independent is to stop relying on the boundaries (or lack of boundaries) others have set for you, and to be responsible to set your own boundaries. Mature and responsible adults know they need appropriate boundaries, and they are willing to follow through and set them. If you don't learn how to set your own boundaries, someone else will impose theirs on you, and that may not always be a good thing.

In their landmark book *Boundaries: When to Say Yes, How to Say No to Take Control of Your Life*, Drs. Henry Cloud and John Townsend write, "The earlier the child learns good boundaries, the less turmoil he or she experiences later in life."[1]

They also say that after childhood, there are two additional periods of life where a focus on boundaries is important.

> The first is adolescence. The adolescent years are a reenactment of the first years of life. They involve more mature issues, such as sexuality, gender identity, competition, and adult identity. But the same issues of knowing when to say yes and no and to whom are central during this confusing time.

> The second period is young adulthood, the time when children leave home or college and start a career or get married. Young adults suffer a loss of structure during this period. There are no class bells, no schedules imposed by others, and a great deal of very scary freedom and responsibility, as well as the demands of intimacy and commitment. This can often become an intense time of learning more about setting good boundaries.[2]

However, the unfortunate truth is that many of us have never really learned what setting good boundaries looks like. We only know the chaos resulting from unhealthy boundaries or no boundaries at all. For many of us, the only boundaries we were raised with were...

- strict and controlling
- inconsistent

- unreasonable
- violated

Healthy boundary construction is essential in the early years of life. But if you didn't experience those essential life lessons in a healthy way, that doesn't mean you're destined for a life of stress and unhappiness. You might have to work a bit harder to get back on track, but it's not impossible. The Bible says in Luke 1:37, "No word from God will ever fail." In other words, *nothing* is impossible with God. The lack of good boundaries in your childhood is no excuse for not learning how to implement good boundaries now while you're on the edge of adulthood.

> The lack of good boundaries in your childhood is no excuse for not learning how to implement good boundaries...

Physical Boundaries

Physical boundaries are necessary to protect your body, your sense of personal space, and your privacy. They help you make decisions about clothes, shelter, safety, money, space, noise, and many other things.

Your physical boundaries need to be strong in order to protect you from harm. As an illustration, if you have a deep wound and it goes untreated, you expose yourself to infection, which can have life-threatening consequences. By applying an antibiotic, bandaging the wound, and protecting it from further trauma, you are creating boundaries. These allow the healing process to take place, and they prevent the wound from doing further damage to your body through the poison of infection.

Likewise, other physical boundaries are essential for your health and well-being.

Distance is a physical boundary. Has someone ever approached you to discuss an issue and stood too close? Your immediate reaction is to take a step back in order to reset your personal space. This sends a nonverbal message to the person that when he or she stands so close, you feel an invasion of your personal space. If the person continues to move closer, your next step might be to verbally protect your boundary by asking him or her to stop crowding you. You're protecting your personal physical space by setting your boundary.

Some teens don't know how or when to take a step back. Some are afraid to even try.

Here are some other examples of physical boundary invasions.

- inappropriate touching, such as unwanted sexual advances
- physical abuse, such as pushing, shoving, slapping, punching, or beating
- looking through another person's personal letters, documents, locker, backpack, purse, dresser drawers, and so on
- not allowing others their personal space, such as barging into the bathroom at home without knocking

Can you see how having physical boundaries in place ahead of time can prevent the negative consequences of not having them?

Psychological Boundaries

Just as physical boundaries define who may touch you, how someone may touch you, and how physically close you will allow someone to be, psychological boundaries define where your feelings end and other people's begin. Many people—adults as well as teens—have little or no understanding of this differentiation.

> When you have weak psychological boundaries, you are like someone caught in a hurricane with no protection.

Psychological boundaries protect the thinking part of who you are—what you put into your head and what goes on inside there. This is the realm of your emotions and thoughts, your will, intellect, worldview, and pattern of thinking. It's what you carry in your mind—your knowledge, wisdom, experience, memories, reflections, speculations, vocabulary, and opinions. It includes both the truths that guide you and the lies you have believed.

Psychological boundaries are important. They protect your sense of self-esteem and your ability to separate your feelings from the feelings of others. When you have weak psychological boundaries, you are like someone caught in a hurricane with no protection. You expose yourself to being controlled by others' feelings, and you can end up feeling bruised, wounded, and battered.

Most of us don't even realize our negative habits that keep us from establishing boundaries. As a teen mother, I carried a lot of emotional baggage, and the older my son and I both got, the more baggage I collected.

Can teens really have emotional baggage? Absolutely.

And you know what? A great deal of this baggage stems from how you think.

But here's the good news—*you can control how you think.*

3

It's All in Your Mind

You are most likely reading a book on setting boundaries because you want the overwhelming pressure of stress to go away. You want your pain to stop. Fortunately, it can!

Life can change dramatically for you when you begin to take ownership of your thoughts and to view your attitude, behavior, and choices from a different perspective. You no longer passively accept whatever life throws at you. Rather, you determine your life's direction.

Perhaps you're reading this because you know you have trouble controlling your negative thoughts, attitudes, or behaviors. Or maybe someone in your life has noticed your frustration and pointed it out to you. Somehow, you've come to the realization that you don't have to continue on your current path, that you're ready and able to change your actions by changing the way you think.

It really doesn't matter what is motivating you to desire change. What matters is that you listen to the conviction in your heart and make the changes you know are necessary.

> It's good to have a wise and trusted adult in your corner.

And it's important to know that when you begin to make choices to change your thoughts, attitudes, and behavior, your life won't suddenly turn into a Disney movie. In fact, sometimes things can get a little rocky because people are used to the way you are. They will have to adapt to the changes in you. Many people don't like change—even when others step out and make decisions for the better.

That's why it's good to have a wise and trusted adult in your corner—a parent, relative, teacher, guidance counselor, therapist, youth group leader, or pastor. It's good to have someone you trust watching your back—someone you can talk to about the changes taking place in your relationships and about the new choices you plan to make.

The Ages and Stages of Life

Although we continue to learn and change until we die, certain physical, emotional, and psychological changes typically take place during the first four stages of life. I'm not going to spend a lot of time explaining the stages of development, but I think it's important for you to understand that boundary development is essential in the early years of life. The most beneficial habits you can develop are to make intentional choices to *think* positively, develop positive characteristics, and have positive attitudes.

Look closely at the years associated with these stages. Clearly, you are going to spend the majority of your life as an adult. Doesn't it make sense that you would want to take every opportunity now to learn positive habits that will contribute to your success and happiness in the future?

- infancy (1–2)
- childhood (3–9)
- developmental stages of puberty (10–13)
- adolescence (14–18)
- young adult (19–29)
- adult (30–39)
- middle age (40–60)
- old age (60 plus, including varying stages of independence to dependence)

It's Your Choice

You *can* shift your thinking, learn new values, and change your thoughts, attitudes, and behavior. And this can be as easy or as difficult as you choose to make it.

My issues as a teen weren't the same as those you face today, but they were significant in my life, and they all brought their share of intense feelings and emotions. I remember feeling afraid, insecure, inadequate, and worthless. I often felt alone and unloved.

Perhaps this is not so different from what you're feeling today.

However, you have something I didn't. You have a resource that is encouraging you to look at the big picture of your life and make smart, intentional choices while you're still a young woman. You have a guidebook in your hands that gives you the power of possibility, and this is your moment to steer your life in a positive direction.

If you're willing, you can be the game changer in your own life. You can begin today to set a course that will result in amazing things in your future.

Here's the real scoop on what you need to know about setting healthy boundaries and making smart choices:

- God loves you, and He wants you to make smart choices.
- God has a plan for your life, and He can heal any hurt you have.
- With God's help, you can overcome *anything*.
- The choices you make today will contribute to who you become tomorrow.
- You can choose how you think, feel, and behave.

The Bible says, "Do not conform to the pattern of this world, but be transformed by the renewing of your mind" (Romans 12:2). Are you ready to renew your mind?

The Choices Other People Make

You control your thoughts and attitudes, but there is no denying that sometimes bad, confusing, and painful things happen that are totally out of your control. When those things happen, maintaining positive and healthy thoughts and attitudes can become very difficult.

> No matter how positive you are, you can't always stop bad things from happening to you.

The fact is, no matter how positive you are, you can't always stop bad things from happening to you. But with the help of a healthy boundary, you *can* change the way you respond to these bad things. You *can* learn how to stop feeling guilty, ashamed, or responsible for these things. And you *can* learn to stop feeling the bad things in such a powerful way.

You Hold the Power to Change

Your teenage years bring many changes—not only physically but also mentally and socially. During your adolescent years, you increase your ability to think abstractly. You're also beginning to make plans and set long-term goals. Everyone progresses at her own rate and has her own view of the world. But generally speaking, these are some of the abilities that become evident in adolescence. Do any of them apply to you?

- develops the ability to think abstractly and independently
- is concerned with philosophy, politics, and social issues
- sets goals
- compares one's self to one's peers
- develops long-term thinking

As you practice abstract, independent, and long-term thinking, you may sometimes think or feel that your choices are incredibly limited. But consider this. Even having the thought that your choices are limited is *a choice you make*.

Every thought you think is a choice you make.

On the surface this may sound like a no-brainer. However, have you ever said or thought…

- She makes me so angry!
- He makes me feel stupid.
- They make me feel worthless.

The truth is, no one can make you think or feel a certain way about anything, no matter how hard they may try. Only *you* can choose how you are going to think about something. Only *you* have the power to control the gray matter that is your brain. She does not really have the power to make you angry. Anger is *your* response. He doesn't make you feel stupid. *You* interpret his actions or words in a way that makes you feel stupid. They don't make you feel worthless. *You* feel worthless only as *you* choose to believe their words.

Therefore, unless you are dealing with mental health issues that prohibit you from cognitive thinking (such as a bipolar disorder or clinical depression) the fact is that *you can choose* to be positive or negative. You can be optimistic or pessimistic regardless of what is going on around you, regardless of what others are saying or doing. In short, your thoughts can be...

- positive (optimistic)   • negative (pessimistic)

Unfortunately, a great many negative people and things influence your life as a teen, and expectations can be overwhelming. It's easy to get caught up in the storm of what is going on around you. That's why it's critical for you to understand the power you have to influence your own life by accepting responsibility for the way you think.

> It's critical for you to understand the power you have to influence your own life by accepting responsibility for the way you think.

This sounds so basic. But I was able to fully grasp and own this fact only after years of counseling and therapy—and I know I'm not alone.

How It Works

Let's look at the way your thoughts naturally progress. Your thoughts lead to attitudes, and your attitudes influence your behavior. Your behavior has consequences.

Your attitude is kind of like a habit—it's your usual way of doing things. Your attitude is how you approach a person, an idea, a situation, or an object. Your attitude is the driver—the decision maker. Successes and failures in life depend on your attitude. If your attitude is generally positive, most of your relationships will be positive. And positive relationships are necessary for a successful life.

In a healthy society, we are rewarded for positive attitudes and behavior, and we are punished for negative ones. At least that is how it is supposed to work. Just like your thoughts, your attitude can be...

- positive
- negative

Pretty much everything in your life starts with your thoughts—positive or negative thoughts, good or bad, happy or sad, healthy or unhealthy—*you* ultimately control all of your thoughts. Likewise, you also control your attitude and behavior. We might represent this as an equation:

your thoughts + your attitude = your behavior

That's a whole lot of control. What are you doing with it?

Here's a powerful secret. *Everything in life will get better if your thoughts and attitudes get better.*

And you can *choose* to make them better.

The Visual Truth of Choices

Your thoughts and attitudes exist primarily inside your head and heart.

Your behavior is the *external* manifestation of your *internal* life. Your behavior is what people see. Your behavior is how you...

- act
- react
- respond

Have you ever stopped to wonder why people behave the way they do? What makes people respond so differently to the same situations?

Often, these differences can be traced to the foundation of a person's values and character—the person's distinctive mental and moral qualities.

There are many things that build and define our character—that make us behave as we do. Generally speaking, the manner in which people behave can be categorized in two ways:

- ethical behavior (acceptable)
- unethical behavior (unacceptable)

Ethical behavior includes characteristics of kindness, honesty, integrity, sincerity, fairness, and equity in interpersonal and professional relationships. That means you treat others as you want to be treated. Unethical behavior is pretty much the opposite, with characteristics like selfishness, cruelty, dishonesty, lying, insincerity, unfairness, and inequality.

Which character traits best describe you? Are you happy with the kind of behavior you typically exhibit? If not, are you willing to change?

Have you ever blamed other people or situations for your attitude and behavior?

Have you ever said or done something that made you feel guilty or ashamed?

Candice often blamed uncaring and insensitive people for her negative attitude and unacceptable behavior. But in high school, she realized that she wasn't happy with her own increasingly negative behavior, and she made an intentional choice to change. This is her story.

> When you're overweight in high school, you have some choices to make if you want to survive. You can permit your self-consciousness to permeate everything and set yourself aside as a loner, a loser, and the butt of jokes. You can also flip it completely around and be the one making the jokes before they have a chance to get to you. I chose the latter.
>
> People in recovery have a saying: "Fake it 'til you make it." It became my mantra. I plastered on a big ol' smile even when it wasn't really appropriate, cracked sarcastic comments from the back of the classroom, and kept everyone in stitches. Before long, and to my surprise, I wasn't just treading water and surviving in the high school shark pool—I was actually popular!

I still felt out of place inside as I shopped with my friends from the cool crowd and they picked out cute, tiny clothes. They didn't make a big deal out of my large size. They laughed almost as hard as I did when I would pick up a top I couldn't get my left arm into and pretend it was a sausage casing. When I was alone, I picked up what fit me in the fat girls' department without an audience.

I joined the choir, the pep squad, the school newspaper. I ran for student council and won. All the while, I'd take a deep breath and survey the state of my performance. If they only knew how I really felt inside! What would happen if I dropped the comedy act? I didn't want to think about it. It was what I had perfected and what they expected from me. Without it, I was just another fat, miserable kid sitting in the corner. Just me, and not nearly good enough.

By the time I was a senior, I was the coeditor of the yearbook and had a lot on my social plate—more than I ever dreamed of and none of which I wanted to lose. Being an upperclassman had also given me a big head. It was around then that my defensive humor took a different turn. I started targeting other people and their weaknesses: skinny legs, crooked teeth, body odor. And people laughed even harder than before. Most of them, anyway.

Quietly, stealthily, almost invisibly—a girl who'd been a friend of mine all the way through school began ducking me in the hallways and stopped returning my phone calls.

"Hey, where have you been hiding?" I cornered her at her locker one afternoon after choir practice.

She drew in a deep breath and looked at me in a way she'd never done before. She looked disgusted, just the way I sometimes thought people who didn't know me reacted at my flabby arms and too-wide rump. But she wasn't looking at my body. She was looking into my eyes, where my soul was supposed to be.

"Look," she began, "I don't know if this is a good idea."

"What are you talking about?" I was clueless.

"You're changing." She blurted it out. "And it's not good. That new girl with the big nose? She heard you. I saw her crying. It just isn't right, that's all." She slammed the locker door and walked away.

I went home that night and took a good look at myself in the mirror. When had I forgotten how it felt to be different? Why did I think it was so important to fit in and be like everyone else? And what gave me the right to point out the inadequacies of others, to sacrifice them so I could continue to feel good about myself?

I looked into my own eyes, into my own soul. I took a good, long look and finally saw myself the way I really was, the way God made me. Imperfect, like everyone else, but all of us in it together, perfect in His eyes.

And suddenly, I knew I had an important choice to make.[1]

Candice suddenly understood that her negative attitude and behavior were motivated by her fear and insecurity of not being good enough. She realized that everyone is flawed in some way—everyone is imperfect. But she also realized that in God's eyes she was perfect just as she was, and suddenly she began to see the world and her choices in a different light.

Candice began to understand the meaning of ethical versus unethical behavior, of being kind versus cruel, and of taking responsibility for her choices. She began to understand her role in the equation.

your thoughts + your attitude = your behavior

In part, Candice had an epiphany because a friend was able to tell it to her straight. Someone was willing to say, "It just isn't right." It's good to have trustworthy people around to hold us accountable.

Candice had a friend who swallowed her fear and set a boundary with firmness and love. I have a feeling her friend's heart was probably beating out of her chest when she finally told Candice how she felt. But she spoke the truth—she set a necessary boundary for herself—and in doing so, she shined a light on the darkness of Candice's choices.

You may need to change your own actions and behavior, or you may be the agent of change God uses to bring someone else an epiphany as they watch you change your reactions and responses to their behavior.

Either way, just remember, a change of perspective and attitude—a personal epiphany—can happen in an instant. And it might come as a surprise to us, but it's no surprise to God.

What's It Gonna Be?

You are incredibly special, and God has placed you in this very moment for such a time as this. God wants you to fulfill His purpose for your life. He wants you to have new understandings—of yourself, of boundaries, of Him, of the Word (the Bible), and of your identity in Christ.

You can decide right now if you want to be...

- a status-quo girl
- a lemming in a sea of lemmings
- a significant influence on yourself and others
- a game changer in your life

What kind of woman do you want to be? Do you realize you're only a few short years away from becoming that woman? Who will she be? You are shaping that woman now. Today. And you get to say what kind of woman she'll be. With God's help and your willingness, you have the power to determine the thoughts and attitudes that will allow you to be the wonderful woman God intends for you to be.

And you can begin today.

Take some time now (if possible) to write in your journal. What do you think and feel about what you have just read in this chapter? Make sure to put the date at the top of the page.

> For the Spirit God gave us does not make us timid, but gives
> us power, love and self-discipline (2 Timothy 1:7).

4

Just Say No to Stress and Yes to Love

When we become overwhelmed with stress, it's often because our yes and no responses are out of balance and coming from wrong or negative places. Consider this. If you're feeling the enormous pressure of stress now at your age, imagine what it's going to be like in the future if something doesn't change. That's why it's critical to learn how to say yes and how to say no—with authenticity, firmness, and love.

The Bible often encourages us to be clear about our yes and our no. Here are two examples.

- "Just say a simple, 'Yes, I will,' or 'No, I won't.' Anything beyond this is from the evil one" (Matthew 5:37 NLT).
- "Most of all, my brothers and sisters, never take an oath, by heaven or earth or anything else. Just say a simple yes or no, so that you will not sin and be condemned" (James 5:12 NLT).

Alas, nothing is "simple" about saying yes or no. These responses are almost always tied to deeper emotions, motivations, and habits.

The most basic boundary-setting word is *no*. It lets others know that you exist apart from them and that you're in control of you.

"Just Say No" was a slogan created in 1982 and

> The most basic boundary-setting word is *no*.

championed by First Lady Nancy Reagan during her husband's presidency. It became a successful advertising campaign as part of the United States' war on drugs during the 1980s and early 1990s, intended to discourage children from engaging in illegal recreational drug use by offering various ways of saying no. In the '80s and '90s, Just Say No clubs popped up all around the country, and school-run anti-drug programs soon became common. Young people made pacts not to experiment with drugs. Eventually, the campaign expanded, encouraging kids to Just Say No to violence and premarital sex as well.[1] Today, the phrase has become a familiar part of our national vocabulary. However, just saying no isn't as easy as it sounds, especially if you didn't develop the fundamental building blocks of security, identity, and love when you were growing up.

And saying yes from a truly authentic place can be just as hard. Have you ever heard your mouth say yes but your inner voice was screaming, "no way"?

Jessica spent years saying yes for all the wrong reasons. She was afraid to say no. But life's demands became so physically and emotionally overwhelming, she could no longer function normally. Shortly before her seventeenth birthday, a girl in her class posted negative things about her on Facebook. This led to a group of girls "unfriending" her, and she eventually had an emotional breakdown.

> I grew up with a mom and grandma who said yes to everything, and in my eyes they always seemed completely capable of doing it all—sewing a quilt for a new baby at church, baking a homemade pie for a sick neighbor, volunteering at a church, or assisting on the PTA at school. It never dawned on me that either of them were unhappy with their choices until I learned years later that my grandma's heart attack was brought on by physical exhaustion and that my mother suffered from chronic anxiety. I learned as a little girl that saying yes wasn't just expected of me, it was the only way to get love, approval, and acceptance. I was so afraid of ever saying no, I sacrificed my health with my "disease to please."

A guidance counselor at school learned of the cyberbullying that was taking place on Facebook, and she intervened on Jessica's behalf. She worked with Jessica's mother to help find a licensed Christian counselor who could help her address the painful emotions and develop the confidence she needed to say yes from an honest and authentic place, and no with firmness and love.

The Truth About Authentic Love

Laura is 15 years old. Her parents are divorced, and she lives with her mother and younger brother. Her dad lives in another state, so she doesn't see him often. Her mom works full-time as an administrative assistant, and her family regularly attends church. Laura and her brother have been raised with clearly established boundaries. When she's confused, she knows she can talk it out with her mom and pray about it until she feels peaceful and right about her decision—her choice. She makes mistakes sometimes, but for the most part, she makes smart choices.

Laura has a strong foundation of faith and a healthy sense of her individuality and identity. She knows when to say no, and she has a standard on which to base her yes.

However, Tiffany's parents are still married, but not happily. Her dad works a lot of hours as a plumber, and her mother is a stay-at-home mom. Tiffany is 13 and has a younger brother and an older sister, both of whom are out of control and rebellious. Like Laura and her family, they go to church, but Tiffany's dad says the only reason they do so is to "keep the pipeline open to get customers." They seldom practice what is preached. Her parents shout and swear at one another, and her sister sneaks out of the house at night. Her mother says that her father only loves money, and her father says that her mother only loves the things his money can buy for her. Tiffany's parents have separated several times, and she lives in almost constant fear of being abandoned. There have never been consistent boundaries in her life, and she longs for stability, structure, and safety.

There is a great deal of confusion in Tiffany's mind and heart regarding what true (authentic) love really is. She often says yes to hurtful people and unhealthy things. She says yes to gain approval and to fit in—even when she really doesn't want to. She doesn't have a healthy standard on which to base her yes and no boundary decisions.

She is very different from Laura.

Setting Your Standard

When it comes to measuring your choices, what standard do you follow?

> Just like gravity, God's love doesn't change, and you can trust in His wisdom to measure anything that happens in your life.

When contractors set a plumb line, they use the earth's gravity. Gravity doesn't change. This is the consistent standard they use for measurement. Just like gravity, God's love doesn't change, and you can trust in His wisdom to measure anything that happens in your life.

The Bible tells us in Proverbs 3:5-6, "Trust in the LORD with all your heart and lean not on your own understanding; in all your ways submit to him, and he will make your paths straight."

Ask God to help you set your standards and identify where you might need to set boundaries. Ask Him to give you wisdom about the issues you are facing today, about the things that might be weighing heavy on your heart.

Look to God as your gravity.

Where All Boundaries Begin

Now is the time for you to decide what your standards will be. What plumb line will you use to measure your value and worth? What's off-limits, and how do you wish to be treated by others? Whom will you hang out with? What kind of influences will you allow in your life, and what kind of an influence will you be on others? What would Jesus really do in your situation?

As a teen, my plan was to meet my soul mate, get married, and live happily ever after. I know it sounds totally hokey, but I really did believe in the fairy tale. I thought a husband was all I needed to be content. I was so unhappy and felt so unloved, and there was no one I felt I could talk with about it—until I met Jerry.

I was looking for love, looking for someone to save me from fear, insecurity, and loneliness. I wanted someone to help me deal with the pain and problems I had been ignoring. I thought Jerry was that person.

I should have set an immediate boundary the first time he hit me. But I didn't, and the violence escalated. Unfortunately, the fear of increasingly violent consequences set the course for many choices I made. My yes and no responses were totally out of whack.

Even when I was finally free of Jerry, I continued to look for a guy to rescue me and love me. What the heck was the matter with me?

If I had spent half as much time and energy searching for God as I did searching for a man, my life would have been much happier and far more fulfilled. I came to a major turning point when I realized I had turned the guys in my life into idols, looking to them to give me meaning and purpose.

It took me a lot of years and a lot of heartache to learn the truth—that there is only one Savior, and it isn't a boyfriend, a baby, or bling. It isn't drugs, an ideal weight, or any person, place, or thing. Only God could fill the God-shaped place in my heart. Only God could give me the love I needed.

Unfortunately, I had a distorted definition of love.

How about you? What is your definition of love? Part of the trouble is that when we're teens, we love just about everything. We love our BFF, our new puppy, and our totally rad cell phone. We love that awesome shade of nail polish, we love those shoes, and we love the new song by Katy Perry. We love the clothes our pop-star idols wear, and we totally love the hottie guys from One Direction and in the Twilight movies.

We love so much and feel love so deeply, but when all is said and done, what does love really mean? A famous line from the classic movie *Love Story* says, "Love means never having to say you're sorry."

It's one of the all-time greatest love-story movies ever made, and although I was a teen when it came out, I remember thinking how absolutely ridiculous that line was. Even then, I knew that nobody is perfect and sometimes an apology is necessary. No way was that the meaning of love.

So then, what is love?

The Face of True Love

A great many things in the Bible are subject to interpretation, but this isn't one of them. Scripture has a definitive answer for this question.

God is love. And because He is love, we can be forgiven, accepted, and saved for eternity.

I've come to realize that setting healthy boundaries is first and foremost about love—the love God has for us, the love He wants us to have for our own lives, and the love He wants us to share with others. Putting the principles in this book into practice will help you see that boundaries are biblical—that in His compassionate love for you, even Jesus set boundaries. Even more important, it will bring you closer to the God who wants nothing more than to hold you in the palm of His hand and love and protect you in every one of your circumstances.

> Setting healthy boundaries is first and foremost about love…

And so we know and rely on the love God has for us.

God is love. Whoever lives in love lives in God, and God in them. This is how love is made complete among us so that we will have confidence on the day of judgment: In this world we are like Jesus. There is no fear in love. But perfect love drives out fear, because fear has to do with punishment. The one who fears is not made perfect in love.

We love because he first loved us (1 John 4:16-19).

Life is filled with countless twists and turns. You have opportunities every day to say yes to God. If you think you need to be skinny, to be perfect, or to have a 4.0 GPA, a guy, a child, a killer career, or lots of money to be complete, I hope you'll rid yourself of those lies before they rob you of true love and fulfillment.

All you need is God's love. And right now you already have everything you need to find it and claim it. You have the love of God. He is on your side as you grow into womanhood. Look again at these first lines from the Bible quote above: "And so we know and rely on the love God has for us. God is love. Whoever lives in love lives in God, and God in them."

Love Is All You Need

A little love goes a long way. It makes people reach out to those who have hurt them, pray for those who don't want it, and forgive when logic says not to. In fact, nothing is logical about love—on the surface, that is. But love is more than a concept or a warm fuzzy feeling in the pit of your gut. Love is choosing to do the hard thing because it's the right thing. Love isn't just doing what Jesus would do, but letting Jesus do through you what needs to be done. Love is believing you are worthy, capable, and precious in God's eyes—just as you are right this very minute.

Will you choose to love that extravagantly? Jesus did, for you.

Why did He do that? *Because you're worth it!*

If it is His will, God will one day bring your knight in shining armor, who will love, honor, respect, and provide for you. But in the meantime, you don't need to look for a man to make you whole. Let God do that. It's His specialty.

Spend your precious teenage years just being a teenager as you allow God to mold and shape you into the awesome woman He wants you to be.

When you desire to make smart choices and change the way you think, feel, and respond, all you need to do is pray for God to help you—to give you wisdom and understanding—and then to turn to the number one bestselling book in the world for guidance, the Bible.

Now, grab your journal. Identify one thing you can do this month that will bring you closer to God. Are you willing to do it? If not, what would help you become willing?

> For the grace of God has appeared that offers salvation to all people. It teaches us to say "No" to ungodliness and worldly passions, and to live self-controlled, upright and godly lives in this present age (Titus 2:11-12).

5

The Center of Balance

I grew up going to the Ringling Brothers and Barnum & Bailey circus every year as a child. The tightrope acts fascinated and terrified me. Every step was intentional, deliberate. And a firm grasp of the balancing pole was essential if the performer was to get safely from one side to the other.

We are walking on a tightrope every day of our lives. So let's think of God as our balancing pole. When we firmly grasp God's principles, plans, and purpose for our lives, we can securely put one foot in front of the other and make it safely to the other side of any trial, tribulation, or turmoil. With God and His standards at the center of our lives, we can do anything.

> With God and His standards at the center of our lives, we can do anything.

The Marriage of Balance and Boundaries

We often hear that the key to happiness and good health is to live a balanced life, but what does that really mean? As a kid, you most likely heard about eating a balanced meal—selecting from all of the basic food groups. As you got older, you heard about balancing work and play. This is a huge issue in the lives of countless adults around the world. Perhaps you've already experienced it in your own family.

Actually, to be healthy emotionally and spiritually, you to need to learn how to balance many things—your schedule, family, friends, relationships, responsibilities, career, hobbies, leisure time, weight, checkbook, budget…and the list goes on and on and on.

But seriously, what teen thinks about all of that? It's hard enough to balance schoolwork, friends, and Facebook. Yet trust me, if you can wrap your brain around the concept of balance and boundaries during your adolescent years, I guarantee that you will have far less drama, chaos, and crisis in your adult life. In fact, when you can say no with firmness and love, and say yes from a place of clear identity and calm authority, you will be light-years ahead of many others.

The Pie of Life

My good friend Dr. Debra Peppers is an international speaker who for ten years hosted a three-hour radio talk show called *Shakin' the Salt with Dr. Peppers*. She is also the author of *It's Your Turn Now!*, a powerful book about her 100-pound weight loss and amazing journey from being a high school dropout to being named Teacher of the Year.

Debra believes, as I do, that the decision to find balance in life is one of the smartest choices we can make. But like me, she was once unsure what that meant, causing her to dig deeper until she came across a description of the six primary components that make up our lives. Being a teacher, Debra developed a helpful visual aid that she uses in her book and also in many of the inspirational and motivational talks she gives around the world.

This simple but enlightening diagram includes six pie-shaped slices that clearly identify the areas of life we need to balance. She calls it Life's Balance Wheel. I call it the Slice-of-Life Balance Pie. Debra has graciously allowed me to share her diagram as well as insight from her book.

SLICE-OF-LIFE BALANCE PIE

Before meeting Debra and reading her book, I had never seen a diagram like this. I had never considered all the areas of who I was—I had never looked at all the components that actually made up my identity as a human being.

Have you ever looked at your life from this six-slice perspective with God at the center of it all? Most likely, you've been busy with other things, including growing up, going through puberty and adolescence, school, homework, friends, parents, falling in and out of love, and dealing with issues and expectations. That's understandable.

However, there's a lot more to life than what you're already dealing with. Years ago, teens delayed focusing on all of these areas. But to do so today is detrimental to your health and happiness. So let's look briefly at each slice of life to get a feel for what each area is supposed to contain.

Spiritual	Physical
identity and value	health
Bible study	nutrition and diet
prayer	exercise
inspiration	hygiene
Christian growth	safety and protection
Emotional	**Personal Growth**
heart and soul	education
mind and feelings	hobbies
insight	wisdom and knowledge
Family Relationships	**Work/Finances**
biological family	money
family of God	stewardship and volunteerism
friends and neighbors	career

Now grab your journal and write down the first thoughts that come to your mind when you look at the pie graphic and read the list of components. Make sure to put today's date (including the year) at the top of the page. Then take a minute to make an honest estimation of the proportions you currently give to each of these six areas in your own life. How much time do you allocate to each slice of your own balance pie? Ask yourself why it's important for you to begin to understand all of the components that make up a balanced life.

Increasing Your Self-Awareness

In my previous books, I've been writing primarily for women who are your mom's age or maybe even your grandmother's age. I've talked with countless women who have told me without hesitation that the course of their lives was dictated by the choices they made in their teen years.

By intentionally and deliberately looking at your balance pie as a teen, you have an opportunity now to direct and change the entire course of your life.

This is a really big responsibility. Are you ready for it?

> When we are caught up in competition or even the every-day "rat-race" of life, it is hard to step back and take an honest assessment of what matters most in our life. We can be so busy and so intent on being "the winner" or being "the best" or "the richest" or "the thinnest" or "the most popular," that we forget what is really important in our lives—our faith, our family, our friends, forgiveness, and fun![1]

How We Learn About Balance

In Proverbs 22:6, the Bible encourages parents, "Start children off in the way they should go, and even when they are old they will not turn from it."

In a perfect world, the people doing this training would be two high-functioning parents who are emotionally and financially stable, who exhibit healthy self-esteem and self-respect, and who love each other. In a perfect world these people would be watching your back, keeping you safe from harm, carrying the moral and legal responsibility for your welfare and upbringing, and basically guiding your overall development in all six slices in your balance pie.

You are very blessed if you live in that perfect world. Your journey to learn, set, and maintain healthy boundaries will be relatively easy compared to your peers who haven't had a similar upbringing. But the truth is, very few teens today live in a perfect world.

I know I sure didn't.

In today's world, you could be living with happily married parents, but you could also be living with unhappily married parents. Or maybe your parents are divorced, and you split your time between them. Hopefully the divorce was amicable, but for many kids that isn't the case, and a bitter divorce is often a constant source of bickering, anger, and pain. Then again, you could be growing up with a single parent, stepparent, grandparent, foster parent, another relative, or another legal guardian.

Clearly, in today's world, there is a countless variety of parental role models. Your situation probably hasn't been perfect, but that doesn't mean those who are responsible for you don't love you. And it certainly doesn't mean you can't beat the odds and succeed beyond your wildest dreams. On the contrary, God is using what may appear to be unusual circumstances to raise up some pretty awesome adults —yourself included.

When Parents Have Problems

We learn from the influences all around us but especially from our parents.

Unfortunately, in today's world many parents are struggling with their own demons of anguish, addiction, and affliction, and this could be a source of great confusion, fear, and pain for you. If your parents are hurting, you may be hurting as well.

If the slice-of-life balance pie is significantly out of balance in the life of the primary adult in your world, chances are very high that you might have challenges keeping yourself centered and balanced.

For example, my own mother was a kind and loving woman, but as a result of the serious physical and emotional abuse she experienced as a child, several slices of her balance pie were missing completely. Unfortunately, this trickled down to her children.

I was greatly influenced by art, music, creativity, and individual independence at an early age. When I looked at the pie diagram, I could quickly see that I was sorely lacking in emotional, psychological, and spiritual stability. My mother never talked to me about personal things, such as physical changes to expect or anything about sex. We never had the "facts of life" talk about the birds and the bees. In fact, I would never have known what to expect in puberty were it not for a health class in elementary school. Even then I found it all very confusing. Additionally, my mother's choice to avoid addressing the abuse and molestation in my childhood, to pretend it never happened, had devastating consequences.

The fact is, I never talked to my mother or anyone else about my fears, my goals, or the future. I never learned to communicate with a trusted adult about my feelings and emotions.

My mother's issues and emotional baggage were significant. The imbalance in my own life began as a result of the imbalance in hers, and it grew from there. Yet she did the best she could with what she had. I guess we both did.

One of my biggest regrets today is that I didn't know God's plan or purpose for my life during those critical teenage years. When I was your age, no one ever suggested that I place God at the center of my life and consider Him as my Father and Jesus as a trusted friend. If those things had been in place, perhaps I could have been stronger and more courageous as a teen. Maybe I could have broken the cycle of generational family dysfunction.

If one or more of your parents have their own significant issues, please understand that this isn't an open invitation to be disrespectful or disobedient to them. It just means that you have the opportunity to break the chain of imbalance that may be a generational curse. In fact, you may have the chance to show them who God really is and how much He loves them.

For Such a Time as This

There are no accidents in God's kingdom, and He has placed you in this time and place for a purpose. Whatever your circumstances, God is on your side, and He loves you. With God's help, you can turn your circumstances around for good and become more like Jesus in the process. As you become more dependent on God at the center of your life, you can become stronger in character, more sympathetic and loving to others, and kinder to yourself. You can rise above the stress that threatens to wear you down, and you can stop ignoring the pain and problems that deplete your power as a young woman.

> There are no accidents in God's kingdom, and He has placed you in this time and place for a purpose.

The Attributes of God

God is eternal.

God is faithful.

God is gracious.

God is good.

God is holy.

God is infinite.

God is just.

God is love.

God is merciful.

God is omnipotent.

God is self-sufficient.

God is sovereign.

God is transcendent.

God is wise.

6

The Foundation of Faith

I read *Wonder Woman* comic books as a young girl and watched the series on television. I was enthralled by the power Wonder Woman commanded and the self-confidence Diana Prince (her alter ego) exuded. My dream wasn't to grow up and become a cartoon or television superhero—I just wanted to be as brave and fearless as she was. I wanted to be powerful so I could feel safe, significant, and loved.

Growing up, I never felt any of those things. I never had a sense of identity or belonging. In fact, underneath my external confidence, I was petrified of just about everything.

My parents' divorce when I was young left an empty feeling in my heart that I could never understand. The concept of an earthly father who would love and protect me was never a part of my life, and the idea of a heavenly Father was foreign to me.

Looking for a Father's Love

My friend Michelle McKinney Hammond writes primarily for single women. As I read these words from one of her books, they jumped off the page. I grabbed my highlighter and underscored them in bright yellow.

> Many women have grown up with absent fathers; distant fathers; noncommunicative, nonaffirming, harsh fathers; or even abusive fathers. A father's role in a woman's life is

important. But because the importance of a father is over-looked, many men do not take their rightful place in their daughter's life. Dads give girls a sense of identity, belonging, acceptance, and love from a man—before they experience a romantic relationship.

Some women seek the affirmation they needed from their fathers in romantic relationships. Because many women enter into relationships with their girlhood needs unresolved, their adult relationships don't work. Their hearts are after some-thing that can only be provided from another source.[1]

As a teen, my heart was after pure, unconditional love, but for years I looked to the wrong sources to find it.

As a little girl, did you long for a husband one day who would be just like your wonderful daddy? Or like me, do your early memories include a father who was a less-than-perfect role model? Did you grow up not knowing what it meant to have a man love, honor, respect, and provide for you?

Afraid of the Dark

Today, it's no secret I was an abused teenage wife in my first marriage. But for years I was too ashamed and guilty to admit the extent to which I suffered—the level of brutality, humiliation, and violence I experienced at the hands of someone I loved and trusted, someone who was supposed to love, honor, and protect me all the days of my life. Kidnapping, rape, and beating shouldn't be a part of our memories at any time, yet they were a big part of my life as a teenage wife. As might be expected, those years left incomprehensible scar tissue on my life.

Yet the truth is, this wasn't the first time I was the victim of what is now called relationship abuse—when someone we know violates our trust with physical or sexual violence.

When I was a toddler, my mother was hospitalized for a serious illness, and we kids were sent to temporary foster care. A brutal experience at the hands of my temporary foster parent left me physically, sexually, and emo-tionally abused. When I was returned to my mother, I was catatonic for months. I had a distorted view of love and a debilitating fear of the dark that would last until adulthood.

Perhaps like me, you carry a secret of relationship abuse that occurred when you were a little girl. It's unimaginable the damage inflicted on young children, and my heart aches for you if this is something that is still affecting your life today and contributing to your stress.

> Perhaps like me, you carry a secret of relationship abuse that occurred when you were a little girl.

I know what that pain feels like. It colors everything about who you are.

A World of Make-Believe

Growing up, I had a dress-up collection that was the envy of all the neighborhood girls. I survived childhood abuse and molestation by walling off a part of my heart and creating a make-believe, fantasy world.

We lived in the projects, and money was always an issue, but the Salvation Army Thrift Store was a treasure trove of joy for me as a youngster. I would navigate like a child with a Glitter GPS to the prom dress rack, where a quarter could buy a sublime gown, and high heels went for a dime. I owned my first pair of stilettos when I was five. Though they were used and slightly scuffed, they were like Cinderella's glass slippers to me.

When I began to write in grade school, a new world opened up to me. I had a natural inclination to express myself by writing. Drama came naturally to me, and in each play or skit I wrote, I always got to be the princess, queen, damsel in distress, or heroine. Whatever the circumstances, I was always the one to be gallantly rescued by Prince Charming.

Writing those fairy-tale scenarios, I created a world in which everything was perfect and safe, a place where I never had to be afraid. In my world, there was no danger of physical or emotional pain, the gallant knight in shining armor always showed up, and everyone always lived happily ever after.

When I wasn't playing dress-up, I spent much of my out-of-school hours watching classic love stories on television and reading romance magazines and novels. I began to pretend that I lived in a grown-up world of love, longing, beauty, and romance—long before I really knew what any of those things were. All I knew was that I had an empty place in my heart that needed to be filled. I was desperately looking for love.

When an 18-year-old man-boy began to show interest in me, I was more than ready to see him as my knight in shining armor. And when the line between fantasy and reality became blurred, no one was there to guide me, to help me make smart choices. I didn't have a standard to follow, a plumb line to guide me.

A Wolf in Sheep's Clothing

All I knew growing up was that I wanted something different from what my mom had. I saw how hard it was for her, raising three kids on her own. She worked long hours. And she was often lonely and frustrated, especially when money was short and housing issues loomed. I could see and feel her pain. She cried a lot, yet I never heard her complain.

I was convinced that Mom's loneliness, frustration, and fears were due to her need for a husband. I was sure that if she had a man and if we had a father, all would be right with the world. So I vowed that I was never going to be single. I was going to find "a good man" to take care of me and to keep me safe and protected, one who would care deeply for our children and me. We were going to own a house too. No one was going to raise our rent and threaten to evict us.

I began keeping my Mr. Right list very early in life so I wouldn't risk missing him when at last our paths would cross. It was no surprise, then, that as a teenager, I would run away and get married when I met Mr. Right. Except he wasn't Mr. Right at all. Far from it.

At only 15 years old, I wasn't a very good judge of character. What mattered in my mind was that this man represented security to me. I misinterpreted his dangerous need to control me as protection. The traits I initially saw as loving and warm quickly changed. The relationship became a prison, and I struggled for freedom. I now see how my damaged heart and soul caused my perception of him to be skewed. I saw him as who I wanted him to be, not who he really was. And the difference between those two poles was enormous indeed. I spent a horrific year married to a man whose extreme physical and emotional abuse almost killed me.

When I became pregnant, my reality suddenly became crystal clear. I literally escaped with my life. At the age of 16, my world became a roller coaster of childcare, getting my GED, working, housekeeping, paying bills, and learning how to be a mother. In my frenzied life, I buried the pain of abuse. There was no room in my life for anything but the here and now.

Thus I continued the generational cycle that my mom began of raising a child without the benefit of a full-time father—something I said I would never do. As time quickly passed, I was the mother of a broken teenage son whose own dangerous choices continued to escalate—and nothing I said or did seemed to help.

I filled my days with busy take-charge tasks. I filled my nights with alcohol, drugs, parties, and self-destruction. I filled my soul with empty promises and emptier pursuits. Often, I filled the empty God-shaped hole in my heart by filling my stomach with food. This is when my struggle with food and weight began. I gained more than 100 pounds during my pregnancy, ushering in a yo-yo lifestyle of weight loss and gain that would plague me for decades.

I was *so* lost.

Life had not turned out as I expected…as I planned. For years, I succeeded only in making my life worse until I finally admitted that I couldn't do it on my own. Finally pursuing God as my true Father, putting Him at the center of my life, and allowing Him to teach me what authentic true love really is—these things changed my life. They can change yours as well.

> Finally pursuing God as my true Father, putting Him at the center of my life, and allowing Him to teach me what authentic true love really is—these things changed my life.

It All Begins with Faith

I'm don't know where you stand concerning the topic of faith. However, you can probably tell by now that my own perspective on setting healthy boundaries includes a Christian worldview. I always invite readers of all faiths to learn how to set the boundaries they need to survive, but I believe that a firm foundation of faith and trust in God is a critical part of any enduring solution.

The Bible says in Hebrews 11:1, "Faith is confidence in what we hope for and assurance about what we do not see." In other words, faith is literally believing in something you can't always see.

This may be hard to grasp, especially if your exposure to God has been minimal or if you were introduced as a young child to a harsh, angry, or legalistic God.

But consider this. Do you need to understand exactly how an automobile engine works to be able to drive a car? Or how about the technology in your cell phone—do you need to understand how data is transferred before you can send your BFF a text message? Do you need to understand how electricity works before you flip the switch that will give light to your darkness? The fact is, most of us don't understand how many things work, but we rely on them every day nonetheless.

> For a long time I didn't believe in God, but I'm so very thankful He never stopped believing in me.

Faith in God and relying on His love is a lot like that.

We don't always understand it in our mind, and that's okay. We only have to understand it with our heart and rely on it every day. Faith provides us with the strength we need to face whatever comes our way. We need to follow the Nike advertisement and "Just do it."

I didn't have faith in anything or anyone as a teen or in my twenties and thirties. For a long time I didn't believe in God, but I'm so very thankful He never stopped believing in me.

I took a photograph of a plaque on my office wall and used it as the header on my personal Facebook page (www.facebook.com/allison.bottke). It looks something like this.

Faith is not believing that God can,
it is knowing that God will.

Study after study has shown that faith or religious involvement of some sort can build self-worth in teens. Why is that? Faith can…

- help you connect to something bigger than yourself
- provide you with standards to live by
- help you overcome negative peer pressure
- give you a sense of identity and belonging[2]

Never underestimate the value of believing in something bigger than yourself—especially something that can help you develop an unshakeable identity and provide a spiritual standard by which you can live for your entire life.

Something that can show you what true love really is.

7

How to Build a Lasting and True Love Relationship

To be loved and to love others in a healthy way are important. They were important in my life, and they are important in your life too. But often the baggage we pick up along the journey hurts us in ways that undermine our ability to really "get" love. Such things as neglect, abuse, violence, teasing, bullying, or being made to feel worthless can hinder us from discerning what authentic love actually is.

In my own walk, I've come to understand what love looks like through the heart of God. I've come to understand what trusting relationships look like as I've developed a true love relationship with a trustworthy God.

When you have a true love relationship with God, you can rest assured you will never be abandoned or alone. You will always have a home in God's heart. You can know that in God's eyes, you are His child forever. And this security will bring you peace.

> When you have a true love relationship with God, you can rest assured you will never be abandoned or alone.

Because of His great love for us, God advises us in the Bible to "flee the evil desires of youth, and pursue righteousness, faith, love and peace, along with those who call on the Lord out of a pure heart" (2 Timothy 2:22).

God Allows U-Turns

I wasn't even searching for God the night He found me, but He knew how desperately I needed Him, how desperately we all need Him.

One summer evening I was taking a walk in my neighborhood when I noticed people going into a nearby church. I had just broken up with my fiancée, my 17-year-old son was in jail, and my life was once again spinning out of control. Why did it seem as though nothing I did worked out? Why did I feel so worthless? The feelings of utter helplessness and hopelessness, of unrealized dreams, broken promises, and dead-end streets overwhelmed me. I had carried these feelings since I was a young girl.

Suddenly, my legs developed a mind of their own, virtually propelling me up the steps and through the doors of the church. Wanting to be unseen, I made my way up some stairs to the church's balcony. There I sat alone, looking toward the pulpit and a statue of Jesus. His hands were outstretched, and He was looking right at me. Hot tears fell down my cheeks as emotions I could not explain filled my heart and soul.

What was happening to me? Why was I sitting in a strange church, crying like a baby? The pastor began to speak a message about being lost, without direction, without hope, without faith—and how all that could be changed. He talked of how we needed only to listen to the Holy Spirit and ask the Lord Jesus Christ to come into our heart, and He would be there—just like that.

My walk with God started that day, a day that forever changed the course of my life. Suddenly, I wanted to know more about this relationship with Jesus the pastor described.

Over the next decade, the world opened up to me in ways I never could have imagined. Opportunities, experiences, and spiritual illumination didn't make my life perfect, but I began a process of healing and hope, a life of promise where before there had been empty desolation.

I did not "get religion." I made a spiritual connection that turned my life around. I "got a relationship" with Jesus Christ.

How could I have been so blind for so long? I remember thinking. Then I was flooded with gratitude that I finally knew real love—the love of God my Father.

How Fast Can Change Happen?

So how does someone suddenly change? With God's help, that's how! Rest assured, God already has a plan for your life. When I chose to make God an active part of my life, my outlook on life changed, my attitude and behavior changed, my friends changed, my language changed, my way of dressing changed, my habits changed…even my job eventually changed. My outlook on trials and disappointments certainly changed.

However, these things didn't change on their own. They were the result of smart choices I began to make with God's help—not because someone else was telling me to make them, but because I felt in my heart, spirit, and soul that it was the right thing to do. I knew that the changes I was making reflected the standards by which God wanted me to live, and that if I was obedient, He would bless me far beyond anything I could ever ask or dream of.

I chose to love God first, to place Him at the core of my life, and to read, learn, and follow His directions for my life as written in the Bible. True healing and hope are available in the pages of the Bible. Jesus declared, "I am the bread of life. Whoever comes to me will never go hungry, and whoever believes in me will never be thirsty" (John 6:35).

You can make this choice to love God as well.

It's hard to put into words the overwhelming sense of protection I felt when I asked Him into my life. My journey since then has included plenty of trials and tribulations, but it has been void of the emptiness I once felt as a fatherless girl—the emptiness many young women feel today.

Have you been looking for love in all the wrong places?

> When your priority becomes the development of an intimate and true love relationship with Jesus, the sand in the hourglass of your life shifts.

Your Own Wizard of Oz Story

Remember that scene in *The Wizard of Oz* when the Wicked Witch of the West turns over the huge hourglass and the countdown to Dorothy's demise begins? Of course, we all know that Dorothy doesn't die—the only thing that dies is her nightmare. She eventually realizes that she always had everything she ever needed to return home to safety.

You have everything you need to return home to safety as well. It doesn't matter where you are in your journey. What matters is that you can stop living in stress and fear right now, today, this very minute. You can gain freedom from any overwhelming pressure that weighs you down, and in doing so, begin an amazing adventure of self-discovery. When your priority becomes the development of an intimate and true love relationship with Jesus, the sand in the hourglass of your life shifts.

God offers more good advice when He tells us, "Do not be conformed to this world, but be transformed by the renewing of your minds, so that you may discern what is the will of God—what is good and acceptable and perfect" (Romans 12:2 NRSV).

I don't know about you, but for me, conforming to what the world wanted me to be was disappointing, not to mention exhausting.

A New-Life Prayer of Salvation

In my very early days as a new Christian, I clung to a Bible verse that assured me I was on a new course in my life: "Therefore, if anyone is in Christ, the new creation has come: The old has gone, the new is here!" (2 Corinthians 5:17).

Are you ready to say yes to God and be a new creation? To live a new and fresh life? If you would like to know what true love feels like, what authentic love really is, I invite you to say this prayer and ask God to live inside your heart. If you're already a committed Christian, perhaps you can use this prayer to reaffirm your belief in Him and your love for Him.

> *Dear heavenly Father,*
>
> *Thank You for giving me hope and healing. I have been going down the wrong road, and I want to make a U-turn toward You. I want a relationship with Jesus. Please forgive my sins, wrap Your arms of comfort around me, and help me to receive Your everlasting and true love at this moment. I am weary and brokenhearted from the stress in my young life, and I can't cope by myself anymore. I ask You to shine the light of Your spirit on me and free me*

to take the steps needed for help. Protect me as I learn how to set healthy boundaries in my life, and please help me to know and to do what is right.

In Jesus's name, amen.

A Community of Strength and Purpose

Simply attending a church doesn't necessarily mean you have a relationship with Jesus or even a basic knowledge of God or the Holy Spirit. However, having a spiritual family is a vital aspect of growing your relationship with Christ, and it's important to plant yourself in a spiritual house with a spiritual family. Find a good, solid church—people who believe and teach and live by the Bible. A spiritual family that will help you grow in your faith. You may have to visit more than one or two churches to find such a spiritual home.

The Bible says in Psalm 92:12-13, "The righteous will flourish like a palm tree, they will grow like a cedar of Lebanon; planted in the house of the LORD, they will flourish in the courts of our God." A strong life-giving church and youth group provides the right environment and atmosphere for you to find the support and stability you need to sustain a lifetime of following Jesus. And it will help you understand what it means to place God at the center of your life and to nurture the true love relationship that will be the basis for every healthy relationship you will ever have.

> A strong life-giving church and youth group provides the right environment and atmosphere for you to find the support and stability you need to sustain a lifetime of following Jesus.

8

Claim Your Identity—
Understand Your Value

Setting healthy boundaries is all about knowing what you stand for, who you are, and whose you are. Knowing who you are in Christ brings a clarity of conviction that enables you to stand confidently in God's plan and purpose for your life.

It's been said that the hardest part of moving forward is not looking back. The Bible challenges you to "choose today whom you will serve" (Joshua 24:15 NLT). So how do you choose to start every day and face the drama-rama of school and life without falling back into your old familiar patterns? Where do you get your power to cope with stress and survive the onslaught of choices?

I understand that life is not a musical comedy, and very few teens roll out of bed with an overtly sunny disposition and without a care in the world, ready to conquer the day and whatever may come with absolute joy and serenity. (Very few adults roll out of bed that way either.)

Let's be real. You're an adolescent—your body is changing daily, your skin is driving you nuts, your hair won't cooperate, your emotions are all over the place, the expectations others have for you are insane, the pressure of schoolwork is crazy, and the stress of it all combined is overwhelming. In fact, life can go from epic to awful in the time it takes to walk from your locker to class.

But remember, you have the power to change your thoughts, attitudes, and behaviors.

The Bible says, "God has spoken plainly, and I have heard it many times: Power, O God, belongs to you" (Psalm 62:11 NLT). Therefore, your power comes from the Almighty. When you understand your identity and access God's power, you can better cope with whatever stress comes your way and find peace in the chaos of any crisis.

> When you understand your identity and access God's power, you can better cope with whatever stress comes your way...

God's Plan—God's Power

The movie *Bruce Almighty* is full of hilarious scenes and good solid content about faith. In one scene, Bruce Nolan (played by comedian Jim Carrey) asks God for a sign. At the time, he happens to be driving behind a truck that has many signs on it—signs he should be following. This shows the importance of paying attention as you search for God's will in your life. Sometimes the answer is right in front of you.

The most important lesson I gained from this movie is that we all need to learn to see ourselves and others through God's eyes and not our own—that God loves us and thinks we are valuable just the way we are. God tells Bruce, "Stop looking up and start looking in." Everything begins with who we are on the inside—who we believe ourselves to be. He also tells Bruce, "If you want to *see* a miracle, *be* a miracle."

Through God's Eyes

I began to write my first book when I was 35 years old, shortly after I became a Christian. *God Allows U-Turns* started out as a memoir, my story of living without faith and then unexpectedly finding God on the journey. However, by the time *God Allows U-Turns* was actually published several years later, the book had morphed into a collection of true short stories from people around the world, and that one book turned into an anthology of more than a dozen books.

As the title suggests, it's based on true stories of people finding a new direction in life. I'd like to share one of the amazing stories that appeared in *God Allows U-Turns for Teens*, a story that beautifully illustrates the issue of our identity.

If Only I Were Beautiful
Amy Nicole Wallace

I looked in the mirror and smiled.

He'd asked me out. An older guy from my church's singles group wanted to go out with me, a sixteen-year-old junior. He said I was beautiful.

I believed him.

So much so, that after we'd been dating a little while, his opinion dominated everything. Soon I dropped all my church activities because he didn't like them. He was my boyfriend and just wanted to spend time with me. It didn't matter that my mom and dad didn't like him. Or that my friends from church said things weren't right with our relationship.

I didn't care. I'd grown up an ugly duckling and finally felt like a swan. Someone wanted me. Someone who said I was the most beautiful girl in the world.

That same someone ripped away my virginity one night after hearing "no" too many times for his liking.

I didn't feel beautiful anymore. I felt like trash.

But I continued to go out with him. He never tried to force a physical relationship again. Instead, his anger escalated. He punched a wall out, barely missing my head. He damaged the nerves in my arm yanking me out of a car, accusing me of flirting with another guy.

Then he got in my face and yelled, "Don't even think about leaving me. No one else would want you anyway. You're used goods and I'm the best you'll ever get."

I believed him.

Until I moved away to attend a small Christian college in another city. There I met lots of guys who treated me with respect. But none of them ever asked me out.

Maybe my boyfriend was right. I was used goods, no longer beautiful.

I transferred in the middle of my freshman year to a state university back in my hometown. My friends encouraged me to get out and date other guys and not let my boyfriend push me around. So I did. I broke off our two-year relationship and jumped right into another one.

I moved in with my new boyfriend and spent the next few years trying to stay pretty enough to keep his attention. I played intramural basketball, weight trained, and played racquetball in my free time. On top of that, I held down a part-time job and managed to stay on the honor roll.

Anything to make me feel worthwhile, to feel beautiful.

It wasn't until seventeen years later as I sat in my family room surrounded by teens half my age, listening to them talk each week about boys and wishing they were beautiful, that I started to grasp the truth.

No one could make me feel beautiful.

One of the girls talked about her dad. "My dad says, 'You used to be so cute. What happened?'" Tears streamed down her beautiful chocolate skin. She didn't think she'd ever be beautiful.

I knew differently. She was already beautiful. She just didn't believe it.

Another night I posed a question. "What are you trying to get when you dress to impress a guy?"

Their eyes grew wide. I waited.

One of the older girls spoke up, "I like to dress nice. The boys notice and it feels good inside."

"But what happens when he decides someone else looks better?"

"It hurts."

"Yes it does." I read the girls two quotes that God was using to change the focus of my search for attention.

- "No love of the natural heart is safe unless the human heart has been satisfied by God first" (Oswald Chambers).

- "We are not wrong to think we desperately need to be loved. We do. Our need does not constitute anyone else's call but God's" (Beth Moore).

I spent my teen years trying to get someone to love me. Any way I could. I wanted their attention and their words to make me feel beautiful. I took the questions of my heart to any guy who noticed. Do you see me? Am I beautiful?

Sooner or later everyone who answered "yes" fell under the weight of trying to make me feel okay.

What I've finally received in the deepest part of my heart—what I'm learning to walk through with my youth group girls—is that our cavernous need to be loved, to be beautiful, will be satisfied first in God.

Or it won't be satisfied at all.

So we're taking a U-turn together and encouraging each another to take our questions to God, not boys, or anyone else for that matter. It's pretty amazing to see the light in their eyes as they hear God answer their questions with "YES! I see you. You are beautiful. You are Mine and you are loved."

I'm starting to see that light in my own eyes too. I've stopped saying, "If only I could lose a few pounds. If only I were beautiful." Now I remind myself that I am beautiful in God's eyes. His eyes see me first thing in the morning and on bad hair days.

And He still says I'm beautiful.

Take a good look in your mirror. God has much to say. Listen closely. He is enthralled with your beauty.[1]

We Are All Beautiful in God's Eyes

> Others in your life may give love conditionally, but God's love is unconditional.

Are you able to accept the truth that you have precious worth in God's eyes? That God's love is not based on your looks or performance? Others in your life may give love conditionally, but God's love is unconditional. That means no matter what you do, how you look, what you wear, or what your grade point average is, God's love will always be the same. No matter what.

God's love and your identity in Christ never change. But when you don't know how much you are loved by God, you give yourself away to other things and people. You undervalue yourself, and that is not God's plan for your life.

In her book *Seeing Yourself Through God's Eyes*, June Hunt explains the true source of our value.

> It might help to ask yourself, *How is the worth of an item established?* Let's assume you are at an auction. Item after item is presented for sale and item after item is sold—not always to the *same* bidder, but always to the *highest* bidder. To the one willing to pay the highest price.

> Consider this: Jesus paid the ultimate price for you when He came to earth as a man, willingly died on the cross, and paid the penalty for your sins. Jesus Christ as God did not have to redeem you. But He loves you so much—you are so valuable to Him—He willingly paid the highest price.

> Without a doubt, you have great worth in His eyes![2]

The Peace of Identity

Coping with stress and finding any kind of peace in life will be virtually impossible if you don't see your value and worth in God's eyes. The Bible says, "See what great love the Father has lavished on us, that we should be called the children of God!" (1 John 3:1). You will never be without the love and compassion of the Lord your God.

Claiming your identity and understanding your value aren't passive exercises, especially if you're uncertain or confused about God's plan and purpose for your life.

In her book *The Witness Wore Red*, author Rebecca Musser writes about her confusion in the patterns she learned while growing up in a religious cult.

> Perhaps one of my biggest lessons was learning the healthy difference between *passive*, *aggressive*, and *assertive* characteristics of behavior. I think this is one of the great balances necessary for healthy individuals and cultures, and I have considered it carefully. To be passive means you don't stand up for your own rights. To be aggressive means that you stand up for your rights while not honoring the rights of others. Both of these patterns of unhealthy behavior were dominant in our society, with men and women in substantial measure and in all of their relationships. What was missing was assertiveness, as it was predominantly programmed right out of us. Assertiveness means that you stand up for your rights while honoring the rights of others. It is difficult to be manipulated or to manipulate others when you are genuinely assertive, so that was why it was a danger in a culture built on manipulation.[3]

When you know your identity in Christ, you can find the strength and wisdom you need to be genuinely assertive, set healthy boundaries, and walk in ways that bring glory and honor to God. You are not likely to slide into negative self-talk or self-defeating habits when you truly know and *believe* that you are a daughter of the King with a divine birthright and an incomparable identity. Don't miss the vision God has of you and the value He places on you!

> When you know your identity in Christ, you can find the strength and wisdom you need to be genuinely assertive…

Girl Power

I was 16 years old in 1971 when my son was born. It would be another year before my divorce was final and several years before I could stop looking over my shoulder, terrified every time I heard an unexpected noise or went outside.

Fiercely determined to love my son and provide him with everything he needed, I was bitterly angry at God. I decided I would be much better off if I depended on myself.

It was the perfect time in history for me to do just that.

That next year, Helen Reddy wrote and recorded *I Am Woman*, a song celebrating female empowerment. It became a number one hit, selling more than a million copies and becoming an enduring anthem for the women's liberation movement.

It was a time when women began to come together in great numbers to claim their girl-power identities. People finally started seeing the issue of women's rights as an issue of human rights.

As a survivor of brutal violence in my short-lived marriage, I knew firsthand how little help there was for someone like me. Emergency shelters and safe houses didn't exist back then, law-enforcement officers weren't trained to handle the complexities of relationship abuse, and very few (if any) women were talking openly about their experiences.

The ensuing decades saw many changes as women fought hard to define, establish, and defend equal political, economic, and social rights for women. We stood together to advocate for equal opportunities in education and employment and to speak against all forms of gender-based discrimination and abuse. As a result of this collective effort, our society has greatly changed, particularly in the focus to protect women and girls from domestic violence and sexual harassment and assault.

As a young woman living in the twenty-first century, you may find it difficult to comprehend the struggles of the generations of women whose efforts have led to the provision of rights you have today. We have a much stronger identity today as empowered women, and we're no longer considered second-class citizens. But this came at a great price.

Determined to find our identity, many of us chose to fill the empty God-shaped place in our lives with anything and everything but God—resulting in an aching emptiness in our hearts, tremendous guilt in our souls, and a percolating anger in many of our relationships.

I continue to support the empowerment and rights of women, and I have also come to believe that God does the same. Women can experience true empowerment and strength when we are utterly dependent on

God as our heavenly Father—when we depend on the wisdom of God's Word as the standard or plumb line by which we measure our choices and our identity.

It's All Up to You

You may already struggle with the emotional side effects of not setting appropriate boundaries at the appropriate time. You may have felt unable in the past to make healthy choices in some circumstances or relationships, but that doesn't mean you are doomed to continue the same course.

You *can* make the smart choice to stop looking to others to affirm your identity and purpose, bring you security, and fill the empty places in your soul that only God can fill. You *can* learn how to be genuinely assertive in a healthy, God-honoring way.

As you grow stronger in your faith, obedience, and identity, you will begin to flourish in ways you could never have imagined. When you make the smart choice to claim the spiritual identity you have in Jesus and exercise self-control control and self-awareness, you can influence yourself and others.

In fact, you can change your world. And just like Bruce Nolan in *Bruce Almighty*, you may learn that you are likely to see a miracle when you realize you are a miracle.

Identity Wisdom

Take some time to read the following passages in the Bible that specifically address your identity as a child of God. Grab your journal and write down what God is impressing on your mind and heart about this topic. Once again, remember to put the date, including the year, at the top of the page.

1. You have God-given value because you have been placed into a *new family*, where you are unconditionally loved and accepted by God.

   - You are chosen by God (Ephesians 1:4).
   - You are adopted into God's family (Romans 8:15-16; Ephesians 1:4-5).

- You are a child of God (John 1:12).
- You are born again (1 Peter 1:23).

2. You have God-given value because God has changed you on the inside and has given you *new characteristics*.

- You are a new creation (2 Corinthians 5:17).
- You have a new nature (Colossians 2:11).
- You have a new heart (Ezekiel 36:26).
- You have a new Spirit (Ezekiel 36:27).
- You have a new mind (1 Corinthians 2:16).

3. You have God-given value because you've been given a *new life* in Jesus Christ.

- You are redeemed (Ephesians 1:7).
- You are washed (1 Corinthians 6:11).
- You are purified (1 John 1:7).
- You are justified (Romans 5:1).
- You are sanctified (1 Corinthians 6:11).[4]

In the Image of God

If the *real you* has "*Christ in you*,"
the *visible you*
reflects Christ *through* you.
This is your true identity![5]

Identity Prayer

Dear Lord,

Thank You, Jesus, for giving me another day to grow closer to You and to better understand Your plan and purpose for my life. Help me to always remember that the greatest commandment is to love. Help me to always be kind to others and myself, and to never be afraid to stand up for what Your Word says is right.

Thank You for showing me what it means to have my identity in You.

Thank You for shaping me into a person of strong and honest character, for giving me grace, mercy, and unconditional love. Thank You for teaching me how to be genuinely assertive in a way that honors You and brings glory to Your kingdom.

Being Your daughter is an honor and a privilege, and I love You.

Amen.

9

Unpack Your Emotional Baggage

I've talked to a lot of women over the years, and many of them say they wish they had known more about boundaries when they were teens. This is because many women started to accumulate their emotional baggage when they were teenagers.

If you can grasp the basics of boundaries now, as a young woman, you will be light-years ahead of so many of your peers—and even *my* peers. Baby-boomer women have spent decades living in the fallout of weak or nonexistent boundaries. If you learn how to address this issue now, early in life, you can save yourself a whole lot of pain and anguish later.

Three debilitating feelings consistently come up when women have problems setting boundaries. You may already be experiencing these feelings.

- insecurity
- fear
- guilt

The Instability of Insecurity

Feelings of insecurity can overtake even the most emotionally healthy person at times. We can feel insecure for many reasons, but the lack of a strong anchor of self-esteem is often a significant contributing factor.

Insecure people with low self-esteem usually don't value themselves properly. Therefore, they look for external things or people to give them value. They are easily controlled by the way others think and feel about them and act toward them. Remember Candice? She looked to the thin, popular crowd to give her value—until she recognized her mistake and made the smart choice to change.

People with low self-esteem depend on others' approval and recognition and are often fearful of conflict with others, fearful of rejection by others, and fearful of life in general.

Sadly, fearfulness seems to be a pervasive feeling in teenagers today.

The Fallout of Fear

We all need to feel security, significance, and love. When we don't feel these things, we can become afraid. Teen girls and older women fear similar things.

- being rejected
- feeling worthless
- being alone
- being unloved
- being abused
- letting someone down
- the unknown
- change
- being labeled negatively
- appearing selfish or self-centered
- not being a good enough Christian

This list could go on and on, and the older you get, the longer it can become—especially if you don't know how to set healthy boundaries.

I feared a lot of things when I was a teen, but I didn't fear that someone could walk into my school and open fire on me and my classmates. I didn't fear that the person I was talking to online might be a sexual predator, and

I didn't fear that someone at a party might slip a rufie (a date-rape drug) into my beverage.

With the issues facing teens today, it's perfectly understandable to be afraid. However, you do not need to live your life under a cloud of fear. With help, you can retrain your thoughts, attitudes, and behaviors.

Have you ever heard of the Serenity Prayer? If you or someone you know has struggled with alcohol or drug addiction, you may be familiar with this prayer. The Serenity Prayer is the common name for an originally untitled prayer by the theologian Reinhold Niebuhr. It has been adopted by Alcoholics Anonymous and other 12-step programs. This is the part of the prayer that is quoted most often.

> God, grant me the serenity to accept the things
> I cannot change,
> courage to change the things I can,
> and wisdom to know the difference.

There will be always things in your life beyond your control—things you cannot change—and the best way to cope with the stress of those things is to depend on God and put your trust in Him. Pray for the understanding and courage you need to change the things you *can* control—the things God wants you to control in order to fulfill His purpose for your life. And rest assured that you do have a significant purpose for being here, even if you're not yet certain what it might be.

The Guise of Guilt

In proper doses and for the right reasons, guilt can be a good thing. Guilt serves a purpose. If you feel guilty about something you've done, that's a good motivator not to do it in the future. Guilt tells us that our personal actions have consequences.

> Guilt tells us that our personal actions have consequences.

According to an ABC.com news article, "Research shows kids who have a little guilt are better citizens. 'They're getting better grades in school, engaging in more volunteer work, they're less prone to racist attitudes.'"[1]

If someone offers you advice on how to live a guilt-free life, run the other way because that's not something anyone should aspire to achieve. One of the markers of psychopaths is that they don't experience guilt.

However, too much guilt can be paralyzing. Consistently guilty feelings can corrode your emotional state. To continually judge yourself as being wrong isn't healthy. Women carry an enormous burden of guilt when they think, *What if…if only I had…why didn't I…*and I have observed that this guilt often begins in their teen years.

> Life will increasingly spin out of control if you try to be someone you are not.

Life will increasingly spin out of control if you try to be someone you are not and if you base your choices on negative thoughts. Being controlled by negative behavior or bad habits, or by insecurity, fear, or guilt—that's no way to live.

Begin to Unpack Your Emotional Baggage

Making sense of emotions and identifying your needs is crucial if you are to live an authentic, balanced, and God-honoring life. If you are consistently ignoring your emotions and needs, or pretending your pain and problems don't exist, then feelings of stress, self-destruction, depression, or despair are likely to increase.

Make a decision now to unpack your bags.

Grab your journal and make a list of the emotional baggage you would like to get rid of that is causing you stress—negative thoughts, feelings, attitudes, and behaviors you want to unpack. Write the following sentence at the top of the page, and remember to include the date.

> Today I'm beginning to unpack my suitcase of stress. I'm going to get rid of…

For example, let's say a mean girl at school is bullying you. Your list would *not* include "Get rid of the mean girl." This is not addressing the real issue. It would sure be nice if she were gone, and that would definitely give you some relief from the stress she's causing. But the fact is, there will always be mean people, and you will always be at their mercy until you learn how to set healthy boundaries with them and change your responses to them.

So in this case, you might include this on your list of emotional baggage to unpack:

- Get rid of my fear of saying no.
- Get rid of the insecurity that makes me feel it's okay to be bullied.
- Get rid of my guilt and shame and ask an adult for help.

Discovering your identity and mastering your emotions are lifelong processes, and making this list won't magically change your life. But just being able to write down the things you want to unpack is a huge step toward becoming a woman after God's own heart!

It's important to know what you want to get rid of on your journey to discover who you really are, what you truly want, and who God wants you to be.

10

The Secret Power of SANITY

More than 150,000 adult readers have learned about the SANITY Steps I've created to help people set boundaries in their lives. Now it's time for you to get in on the secret and claim this tool for yourself!

Whether you're facing peer pressure at school, a controlling boyfriend who is pushing you around, or an attack from mean girls on your Facebook page, you can decide right now to stop the insanity and shift your perspective on the situation. You can usher in your own epiphany as you repeat to yourself, "I choose sanity, I choose sanity, I choose SANITY!"

If you look up the word "sanity" in your dictionary, you'll find a definition such as "mentally sound, wise, sensible, and rational." Conversely, insanity is the opposite—not mentally sound, foolish, wild, and mad.

According to a popular definition, insanity is repeating the same behavior and expecting different results. Another way of describing it is to envision gerbils and hamsters on exercise wheels that take them nowhere regardless of how fast they run. That's essentially what insanity is, and it's what the person without healthy boundaries is doing—running on a gerbil wheel and going nowhere.

I know that wheel all too well. I spent years running on it—years I will never get back. I long to spare you from making the same mistake.

As painful as this season in your life may be, just think how much worse it can get if you continue to make unhealthy, insane choices into your twenties, thirties, and beyond. Imagine how much baggage you'll be carrying as you get older. Our bad choices seem to have a way of gathering momentum and size, just like a snowball rushing downhill.

The good news is that you don't have to be a victim in a crazy world of gerbil-wheel living—you can choose to be a victor! You can break the cycle! Just say no to the gerbil wheel of excess stress, poor choices, and unnecessary emotional baggage, and yes to SANITY!

> The good news is that you don't have to be a victim in a crazy world of gerbil-wheel living—you can choose to be a victor!

The Setting Boundaries books have been born out of my own experience, though in most of the books I also include stories of others who found their way back to SANITY. Out of sheer necessity, I've walked the walk that led me to write them. The first book in the series, *Setting Boundaries with Your Adult Children*, was a result of the pain I endured in my challenging relationship with my adult son, Christopher. Time after time I bailed him out of trouble, thinking I was helping him. The truth is, I was merely enabling my son to continue his inappropriate behavior. I was also driving myself crazy by trying to keep up the many other demands on my life. It simply wasn't working—at all.

As a result of that sad experience, I developed the SANITY Steps, which helped me gain control of my life and a deeper understanding of God's plan and purpose for my life.

It took me a while, but eventually I made the move I'm asking you now to make: Move off the gerbil wheel of insanity into the world of sanity—using the Six Steps to SANITY.

The Six Steps to SANITY

When stress becomes overwhelming and you need to think fast, act fast, and make a choice that could change the course of your life (or the life of someone else), you're probably not going to have this book nearby or yellow Post-it reminders on hand to guide you.

That's when you need to be able to search your memory bank for a useful tool that will help you navigate through any possible meltdown and make the smartest choice possible. That's when you can picture the word

"SANITY" and quickly apply the step that is most applicable for your situation.

SANITY is an acronym for six specific actions you can take to help you make smart choices when you're faced with multiple options, or when situations and circumstances are spinning out of control. These steps will empower you to change your direction. Following these six steps won't make every bad or painful thing go away. They're not ruby slippers that can magically transport you home from Oz, but they are effective tools that can help you navigate whatever comes at you in a proactive and powerful way.

> SANITY is an acronym for six specific actions you can take to help you make smart choices.

At first I had to consciously think about the six steps—about the process—when faced with difficult choices. Now they are almost as natural as breathing. In time, these steps can become second nature to you. If you choose SANITY over insanity and consistently apply these six actions to your choices, I can assure you that *your life will change.*

S—Stop Ignoring Your Pain and Problems
(Stop, Step Back, Be Still, and Think)
A—Assemble Supportive People
N—Nip Excuses in the Bud
I—Implement a Plan of Action
T—Trust the Voice of the Spirit
Y—Yield Everything to God

By the way, I have a relatively poor capacity to memorize things, but I found it amazingly easy from the beginning to memorize these six steps. I hope you will as well. And here's a big plus—you can apply the six steps in any order to your issue.

For example, Jessie has a BFF who is consistently late. Carrie often doesn't show up at all, and she never bothers to call. When Jessie calls to find out where she is, Carrie acts like it's no big deal and always rattles off a string of lame excuses.

"The last time it happened," Jessie said, "all I could think about was the 'N' step in SANITY—*Nip Excuses in the Bud*. I remembered you writing, 'Excuses are often justification to continue unacceptable negative behavior.' Carrie always had a million excuses why she was late or blew me off entirely, and I suddenly realized that her behavior wasn't acceptable anymore. I didn't deserve to be treated that way, and I had to set a boundary so I wouldn't feel used. I had to *Nip Excuses in the Bud*!"

In Jessie's case, the boundary she set was to tell Carrie how she felt when Carrie stood her up, and to let her know that in the future she wouldn't wait more than 15 minutes before making other plans or leaving without her. Additionally, she had this conversation with Carrie when she wasn't angry or emotionally upset. Bravo, Jessie!

So let's jump right in to the SANITY Steps, shall we?

S—Stop Ignoring Your Pain and Problems (Stop, Step Back, Be Still, and Think)

This first of the Six Steps to SANITY sounds the easiest, yet it is one of the most difficult. They say the first step in any journey is often the hardest. However, without this crucial first step, you will never arrive at your destination—learning how to cope with stress…learning how to STOP the insanity.

Your ability to focus and make smart choices will increase when you can expose the pain, confront the problem, and consistently tell yourself to stop, step back, be still, and think—*before* you get caught up in responding emotionally (instead of rationally) to a challenging situation or choice.

There's a good chance that even now you're stressed because you've been ignoring something painful or uncomfortable, hoping it would somehow disappear or work its way out. Am I right?

Pain is designed to get your attention, and we should never ignore it. Whether it's the physical pain of someone grabbing your arm too tight or the emotional pain of heartache, abandonment, or betrayal, healing can only begin when you expose the pain, confront the problem, and STOP pretending it isn't happening or isn't a big deal.

For example, have you ever gotten a splinter in your finger? It's only a tiny piece of something. But if you ignore it, the chance of infection increases. In a very short time, your finger can swell, change color, fill with pus, and begin to throb. In extreme cases, this can be followed by fever, blood poisoning, and even death. All this would have happened simply because you ignored the initial pain of the splinter and the problem of infection.

The emotional pain you may be feeling is likely to be far worse than the physical pain you'd feel from a splinter, but the analogy remains the same. The longer you ignore it, the worse it's going to get.

For example, just a few hours ago I found myself in an unexpected situation that threatened to send me into a stress-filled meltdown. I was ignoring the physical pain of heartburn and the emotional pain of someone's unrealistic expectations. As the tension increased, I took a deep breath, sat up straight, and literally told myself, *Stop!* I told myself to stop ignoring the pain and the problem, and to step back before I said another word. I stopped the gerbil wheel of insanity from spinning by choosing not to get on it in the first place. This pause allowed me to regroup and think so I could respond rationally and not react emotionally.

> The next time your boyfriend accuses you of something, someone says something mean, or you begin to feel insecure or fearful, tell yourself, *Stop!*

Sometimes, just by thinking about this first step, you will be able to turn things around. I'm serious—try it! The next time your boyfriend accuses you of something, someone says something mean, or you begin to feel insecure or fearful, tell yourself, *Stop!* And then respond in a totally unexpected way.

This first step becomes easier to do the more you come to understand two things—God doesn't want you to live with overwhelming stress, and you have the power to change with His help.

Here's another example of this powerful step in action.

Christy is 14 years old, and she's afraid of almost everything. She's afraid of not fitting in, of being bullied, of being alone, of not measuring up to the popular kids, and of not meeting everyone's expectations. The pain of fear rules her life. And so she has spent years doing her best to fit in, even if it means losing her own sense of identity.

As Christy worked with a counselor to address her fears, a series of self-discovery epiphanies began helping her change her negative thoughts. When her BFF tried to convince her to shoplift from a store in the mall "just for the fun of it," Christy stood up to her fears and set a healthy boundary. She said no. She had never before dared to say no to this bossy friend.

Christy knew shoplifting was wrong, but so were many things she had been doing, like criticizing others, cheating on tests, and sneaking out of the house at night—all because she was trying to fit in.

"All I could think about was the S step in SANITY," Christy said. "And I suddenly realized that I had to stop pretending I was someone I wasn't. This wasn't me. I wasn't a liar or a thief. I had to stop reacting emotionally and start responding rationally. And when I stopped and thought about what my friend wanted me to do, I was more afraid of what could happen if I got caught than I was of not fitting in with the group. I didn't want to get arrested. I didn't want to end up in jail."

When you *Stop Ignoring Your Pain and Problems*, you stop some very specific things. We all have different things we need to stop ignoring, and only you and God know what your particular things are.

So grab your notebook and make a list of the things you feel that God is telling you to *Stop*, things associated with the pain you are feeling and the problems you have. Here's Christy's list.

- Stop being afraid of not fitting in.
- Stop saying yes when I want to say no.
- Stop giving in to peer pressure.
- Stop feeling sorry for myself.
- Stop being mean and nasty to the geek girls at school.
- Stop pretending I'm someone I'm not.
- Stop disobeying my parents.

When it comes to stopping anything, a good tool to use is positive self-talk. After you've identified what you need to stop, you've got to convince yourself that you really can do it.

Remember, wrong thinking releases wrong emotions, attitudes, and behaviors. When you make a decision to have right thinking—positive thinking—you'll need to reprogram your brain. For example, you might say this out loud in private:

> I'm going to **stop** being afraid of what other people think about me. I'm going to **stop** giving in to peer pressure. I'm going to **stop** compromising my own beliefs and start making my own decisions. I'm going to **stop** thinking I'm worthless.

God wants you to enjoy the plans and purposes He has in store for you, and He has empowered you to change your life. The Bible says, "I can do everything through Christ, who gives me strength" (Philippians 4:13 NLT).

> God wants you to enjoy the plans and purposes He has in store for you.

A—Assemble Supportive People

The pain you're feeling and the problems you're having that are causing overwhelming stress *should not be ignored*. It takes a lot to *Stop* ignoring your pain and problems. And it takes even more to reach out and get help—but you can do it!

When life gets tough, it's important to have people nearby who can lend encouragement by listening, praying, and offering advice and an occasional shoulder to lean on. It's vital that you surround yourself with supportive people you trust—people who can give you wise advice and help you navigate your way through the storm. Talk to your parents, a school advisor, your youth group pastor, or a licensed Christian counselor. Or attend a recognized support group. *Just start somewhere.*

Your support may be comprised of one person at first, or just two, three, or four people who are close to you. Just make sure your support person or team will extend healthy advice and share your biblical values. Receiving advice from someone who doesn't share your faith can lead to mixed signals and frustration. And receiving advice from someone who isn't aware of the psychological, emotional, or physical consequences of what they are saying—that can lead to much worse.

If you're dealing with depression, anger, addictions, eating disorders, or the aftereffects of being abused, molested, or raped, it's important to know you're not alone in whatever challenge you're facing. Countless small groups are meeting around the country, and you may find that a support group for your particular issue already exists nearby.

Call the hotline numbers listed on pages 136 and check with area churches, community centers, and nonprofit organizations to find groups that support people who are working through the same issues you are.

For example, 16-year-old Susie cuts herself—not for the adrenaline rush, but as a desperate means of survival. Her emotional pain is so deep and she's ignored it for so long, she's dying on the inside, and the only way she knows she's alive is to feel the physical pain and see her own blood.

This scares her. A lot. Especially now that the razor scars are running like stripes on her arms and stomach. They're getting harder to hide.

Then she saw a flyer on the school bulletin board for a group of cutters that was meeting nearby. She was initially fearful, but the more she prayed about it, she became even more afraid of *not* going. Later she was able to say, "This group helped me to get strong enough to save my own life. It helped me realize that I mattered."

You can also find a wealth of support available on the Internet, but be very careful to exercise clearly defined boundaries concerning online support groups. Never disclose your name, address, phone number, or other private information to people you meet online. Be sure to read chapter 14 on Internet predators.

In some situations, meeting one-on-one with a qualified counselor, therapist, psychologist, or psychiatrist may be necessary. *Never ever be ashamed or afraid to get help.*

Another word of warning. If you're presently in a relationship with an overbearing guy, you may find this step all the harder. A controlling guy may be opposed to or even openly hostile toward your attempts to seek help. He may perceive *anyone* in your support group as an enemy and feel threatened by your whole notion of setting boundaries. If this is the case in your life, choosing to *Assemble Supportive People* is all the more critical.

Please, if someone—anyone—is hurting you, please seek support immediately. You show strength, courage, and fortitude when you ask for help. Break the chain of victimization by declaring your identity as a survivor and a conqueror! Press on with caution. Other young women have been in your spot and have summoned the courage to change, and you can too. In turn, as you heal, you may be able to offer your support to others facing the same challenges you are. In time, your actions can empower and influence other girls to take life-changing steps forward. With that in mind, I've included a short section called "How to Assemble a SANITY Support Group" (chapter 18).

> Please, if someone—anyone—is hurting you, please seek support immediately.

We've also created a special Facebook community just for readers of this book, so make sure to stop by at www.Facebook.com/SanitySupport forYoungWomen and "like" our page today.

N—Nip Excuses in the Bud

Setting boundaries can be fraught with obstacles. Often, those obstacles include excuses—either from you or from the person with whom you've set a boundary. These excuses are often merely justifications of negative behavior.

Many adults have a hard time identifying excuses, so don't be surprised if this takes some time for you to master. The plumb line to use for accurately measuring excuses is to ask yourself, *Is this excuse a justification of a negative behavior—a wrong behavior?* Excuses can sound like this:

"He didn't mean to hit me. He had a rough day at school."

"My BFF isn't involved with drugs. She just got hooked up with the wrong crowd."

"When my uncle hugs me too tight and rubs his body against me, it's just harmless attention."

It is never okay to accept or excuse these negative (wrong) behaviors:

- physical abuse
- sexual abuse or molestation

- verbal abuse
- dating abuse
- psychological or emotional abuse
- bullying
- jealousy or control
- being an Internet predator
- acting in a threatening or violent way

Excuses can sometimes masquerade as accusations. Resist the urge to accept accusations that are really excuses from those with whom you've set boundaries. Plan ahead to respond in ways that clearly establish your yes and no.

I—Implement a Plan of Action

We may not like them, but quizzes and tests are huge parts of going to school. An exam goes with a curriculum that includes action plans—lessons for you and your teacher to follow. Without a written plan of action, you wouldn't know what's expected of you, your teacher wouldn't know what to expect from you, and there would be no tangible way to measure your learning and growth.

A personal action plan is like curriculum for your life—it helps you envision your future and develop positive habits that will enable you to achieve success and live a purposeful life. Implementing a plan of action for your life is a tangible way to see where you're at—and more important, where you're going.

Unfortunately, we often get caught up in our own thoughts, emotions, and choices. Before we know it, we're running full speed ahead on the gerbil wheel of insanity with no clear plan or direction for where God really wants us to go.

This step involves…

- identifying and prioritizing your goals, dreams, and standards
- looking at potential roadblocks or challenging areas

- determining what actions you need to take to implement change
- carefully considering the possible consequences when you begin to make changes

Take some time to begin writing your plan of action. You may be the only one who sees it, but you need to write it out nonetheless. Writing out your plan adds strength and clarity to your resolve. Implementing your plan is all about *taking action*.

When you know where you're headed, you can make smart choices to get there.

T—Trust the Voice of the Spirit

The Bible says in Proverbs 3:5-6: "Trust in the LORD with all your heart and lean not on your own understanding; in all your ways submit to him, and he will make your paths straight."

How does God make your paths straight?

He does this by giving you spiritual wisdom and discernment as you depend on Him. God can lead or restrain you in your decision-making process as you grow your relationship with Him. And that relationship begins with trust.

When we trust in the Lord with all our heart, we must also trust what He teaches us about the power of the Holy Spirit. Jesus told His disciples, "I will ask the Father, and he will give you another advocate to help you and be with you forever— the Spirit of truth. The world cannot accept him, because it neither sees him nor knows him. But you know him, for he lives with you and will be in you" (John 14:16-17).

God has a good life planned for you, but God's ways are not our ways, and it takes time to learn how to operate in His ways. The key to effectively coping with stress is to intentionally develop your faith and learn how to *Trust the Voice of the Spirit*.

> God has a good life planned for you, but God's ways are not our ways, and it takes time to learn how to operate in His ways.

Y—Yield Everything to God

The final SANITY Step is to yield. To "let go and let God." When the letting go part has been accomplished in your heart and letting God has become your focus, something amazing begins to happen. You feel free! You may not even realize how your fears had imprisoned you until those fears are gone.

The process of mending a broken heart from violated boundaries and relationship abuse can take a long time. I know this well. I also know that when we yield, God restores.

Facing the pain of my abuse and the damage it did to my heart, soul, and spirit has taken years. It's like peeling an onion as layer after layer of self-discovery brings new tears and new enlightenment.

To be sure, letting go can be scary. You must let go of unrealistic expectations, negative emotions, and lies of the enemy. When you choose to *Yield Everything to God*, you make a choice that will forever change your life.

The Purpose and Power of SANITY

I've written five books in this series before this one. I've reviewed hundreds of boundary questionnaires and read countless e-mail messages from readers around the world. Most of the people struggling with boundary-related challenges are adults who spent years ignoring their pain and problems—years in bondage to the consequences of poor choices. Adults who finally hit the wall and said, "Enough is enough." Adults whose hearts are bruised, broken, and seemingly beyond help. Adults who desperately want to get off the gerbil wheel of insanity.

I ask you now to consider some questions. These could transform the way you think.

Do you think adults reach a point of desperation suddenly? Does it happen overnight? Or did a gradual and steady progression of poor choices probably began in the prime time of their lives—when they were teenagers who had their lives in front of them? Did they grow accustomed to ignoring their pain and problems? If they had made different choices when they were younger—your age, perhaps—would they be in the same place today?

I'd like you to jot down your responses to the following questions in your journal.

1. What will my life look like in five years? In ten years?
2. How might my life improve if I stop ignoring my pain and problems now?
3. How can applying the SANITY Steps change my life?

Six Steps to SANITY

S—Stop Ignoring Your Pain and Problems

A—Assemble Supportive People

N—Nip Excuses in the Bud

I—Implement a Plan of Action

T—Trust the Voice of the Spirit

Y—Yield Everything to God

---

in·san·i·ty
/in 'sanitē/
n: doing the same thing
and expecting different results

Visit our Facebook community just for *you* at Facebook.com/SanitySupportforYoungWomen

SettingBoundariesBooks.com

11

Under the Dome of Pressure

How do you feel when you're stressed? Most of us get tense—physically and emotionally. We normally feel stressed when we're threatened or anxious. Some stress can be helpful (as when we're preparing for graduation). But it can also be unhelpful (as when it keeps us from effectively dealing with traumatic events or situations).

Everyone experiences stress at times—adults, teens, and children. Stress can motivate you to develop the skills you need to cope with and adapt to new and potentially threatening situations. However, the beneficial aspects of stress diminish when it is severe enough to overwhelm your ability to take care of yourself. You're severely stressed when a cyberbully attacks you on Facebook and makes life so awful that you start to do drugs or sneak alcohol before going to school so you can face your peers.

> The fact is, horrible things are happening all around you, yet many folks expect you to bounce back and be resilient simply because you're young.

Sometimes after a traumatic event that is especially frightening, you might have a strong and lingering reaction. You may experience powerful and painful emotions, jitters, sadness, or depression after an overwhelming situation.

The fact is, horrible things are happening all around you, yet many folks expect you to bounce back and be resilient simply because you're young. However, the reactions from stressful events can be significant and life changing. Have any of your problems resulted in any of these?

- disbelief, shock, and numbness
- feeling sad, frustrated, and helpless
- fear and anxiety about the future
- feeling guilty
- anger, tension, and irritability
- difficulty concentrating and making decisions
- crying
- reduced interest in usual activities
- wanting to be alone
- loss of appetite—or increase in appetite
- sleeping too much or too little
- nightmares or bad memories
- reoccurring thoughts of the event
- headaches, back pains, and stomach problems
- increased heart rate, difficulty breathing
- smoking or use of alcohol or drugs

Are you feeling any of these reactions to negative stress? By using healthy ways to cope and by getting the right care and support, you can put problems in perspective and begin to feel the stressful feelings and symptoms subside. However, this is easier said than done in many cases. If not addressed properly, one reaction can become a series of reactions that can lead to seemingly unmanageable pressure. That can sometimes lead to devastating results.

Extreme Stress

Most teens today know of someone who has committed suicide. Suicide is the third-leading cause of death for youth between the ages of 10 and 24. It results in approximately 4600 lives lost each year.[1]

Understandably, many adults are fearful to address this topic. Some people can't comprehend what it's like to feel utterly hopeless—to be so damaged by past or current events that you're too afraid and too tired to even go on, and so opting out of the future seems to be the best thing to do.

If this describes you, *please don't give up.*

Please believe that your life is precious to God. You were born an original, unique in every way, and God has a specific plan and purpose for your life—no matter how hopeless things may seem right now.

Don't let the enemy win. Don't let the pressure of stress steal your joy and rob the world of your unique contribution.

When you find yourself being attacked by fear and hopelessness, call on God's power to give you strength. The Bible says, "God is our refuge and strength, always ready to help in times of trouble" (Psalm 46:1 NLT).

You can trust that whatever Satan means for harm, God will eventually turn it around and work it out for good. He tells us in Psalm 60:12, "With God we will gain the victory, and he will trample down our enemies."

> Don't let the dome of pressure suffocate the very special person God has created you to be.

Don't let the dome of pressure suffocate the very special person God has created you to be. Instead, claim your powerful identity in Christ and decide right now to take control of your thoughts, attitude, and behavior.

Let's talk about what is causing this paralyzing pressure and stress in your life, starting with unreasonable or unrealistic expectations. Let's begin to replace the insanity with SANITY! Let's STOP the stress!

12

The Exhaustion of Expectations

So many factors make up your humanity. You have been molded by your circumstances, environment, coping styles, experiences, natural-born temperament, influences, and of course by your own choices. You have also been molded by expectations.

Virtually all teenage girls today seem to be struggling with an impossible set of expectations and challenges that threaten to overwhelm them. They are desperate to please their families, teachers, and friends, but societal expectations, cultural trends, and conflicting messages put girls at a higher risk for depression, eating disorders, and suicide.

> Virtually all teenage girls today seem to be struggling with an impossible set of expectations and challenges that threaten to overwhelm them.

These are some of the key areas of exhausting expectations affecting young women today:

- performance (measuring up)
- body image and looks (self-worth)
- school, friends, and parents (in that order)
- dating, sex, and STDs
- social media struggles

In responding to a question on one of our surveys, author Virelle Kidder told about her life-changing epiphany regarding expectations.

> My mother's expectations and emotional neediness controlled our home and much of my life until I was in my fifties. Sad, but true. A Christian counselor straightened me out in one hour by explaining the difference between what God expects of me and what my mother expected of me. Two different things entirely. The relief was immediate. Tears flowed as the enormous weight I'd been chained to forever was loosened.

Virelle had a mother whose expectations were unreasonable.

When you've been repeatedly exposed to unreasonable expectations, or when you develop a highly responsible, performance-oriented mindset, you can easily develop unreasonable expectations for yourself and for others. But God doesn't demand perfection from you. God isn't expecting you to measure up. He's not expecting you to perform for Him. He has never expected you to live the Christian life on your own or meet His holy standards. If He thought you could, He wouldn't have sent Jesus to earth to die for you. But He did.

God wants you to be free from the bondage of expectations, to enjoy the freedom and love of being in a relationship with Him.

God Expects Great Things from You

God loves you just as you are, and He also expects great things from you. God has desires (expectations) for all of us. He has placed a call on your life, something specific for you to do, but you find out what it is only as you go along and trust God. God has a good plan for your life, and He will reveal it to you when the time is right. He will also give you everything you need to fulfill your calling. His desires for you are not burdensome.

It's human nature to want to find meaning in our lives. We are created in God's image, designed to be creative. Yet in our human quest to live up to unrealistic expectations, we can lose sight of what that means.

> What do people really get for all their hard work? I have seen the burden God has placed on us all. Yet God has made everything beautiful for its own time. He has planted eternity in

the human heart, but even so, people cannot see the whole scope of God's work from beginning to end. So I concluded there is nothing better than to be happy and enjoy ourselves as long as we can. And people should eat and drink and enjoy the fruits of their labor, for these are gifts from God (Ecclesiastes 3:9-13 NLT).

It's good when your expectations match God's desires for you, but not so good when they're unreasonable or unrealistic.

The Truth About Expectations

Are you confused about what is really expected of you? Do you feel that no matter how much you work or how hard you try, you'll never be able to achieve all that is required of you? It's difficult to find joy in life when your expectations for yourself and others are out of balance. So let's take a closer look at this. When it comes to expectations, I've found there are three primary types:

- reasonable (justifiable)
- unreasonable or unrealistic (impossible)
- different (individual)

Some expectations are entirely reasonable, such as expecting a friend to be truthful, a teacher to be fair, a parent to be protective, or a guy not to hit you. It's reasonable to expect to receive a paycheck at the end of the pay period or to pass a test if you study hard and do the work. It's also thoroughly reasonable to expect people not to treat you with physical, emotional, or verbal abuse.

However, expectations can become problematic when they become unreasonable or unrealistic. For example, we shouldn't expect toddlers to understand the consequences of their actions— that would be unreasonable. We shouldn't expect habitual drug abusers to respect our personal property—that would be unrealistic. And we shouldn't expect ourselves or others to be perfect— that's downright impossible.

> If we're not careful, unrealistic expectations can set us up for failure and leave lasting scars on our hearts.

Regardless of our age, women have a keen sense of needing to live up to expectations—those from our families and friends, our culture, our Christian community, and those we place on ourselves. We tend to have unrealistic expectations about what we should be able to accomplish and about what life is going to be like. But life usually doesn't follow our expectations. If we're not careful, unrealistic expectations can set us up for failure and leave lasting scars on our hearts.

Different Expectations

People have different expectations of the way respect, loyalty, forgiveness, dependability, work ethic, promptness, commitment, and such things should be expressed in a relationship. For example, I always try to arrive a few minutes early for appointments, but I have a friend who thinks he's being prompt if he's no more than 15 minutes late. Clearly we have very different expectations of what it means to be prompt. It's important to realize that people don't always think alike or share the same expectations. In many instances that's okay.

We can exhaust ourselves by expecting others to respond to situations the same way we would. Have you ever said, "I can't believe she did that! I would never even *think* of doing something like that!" The truth is, we live in a world where people don't always share or live up to our expectations, and sometimes this reality hurts us.

The joy of diversity is a blessing, but our differences can bring some of the most complicated challenges to the surface. Having different opinions, choices, and expectations is natural. However, when our ethical and moral standards are different or are being threatened, it takes courage and conviction to stand up for what we know is right and not lower our expectations because we're being pressured to do so.

Overcoming Worldly Expectations

Daily, young women around the world are threatening their physical health and emotional well-being by trying desperately to align themselves with an image portrayed by the media. We must remember that the media have one main goal—to offer us a false promise of security and worth in order to take our money.

As Christians we have a God who is bigger than any media. But we must call on Him to help us overcome the lies that come our way on a daily basis. God knows the battles we face where the media is concerned. And it is just that—a battle.

> Satan uses this lie to keep us captive, causing us to be self-conscious, depressed, and disappointed with ourselves.

We are easily desensitized by the images we see in the media. We hope against hope to be just like those "perfect" bodies who are living "perfect" lives on the screen or in a magazine. We are easily fooled, yet this is not reality. Satan uses this lie to keep us captive, causing us to be self-conscious, depressed, and disappointed with ourselves because we can't match the media's standards.

There is no quick and easy way to stamp out this dangerous worldly expectation, but we can be aware that the media has their own agenda and that it's quite opposed to God's agenda. I make it a practice to *not* allow the media to influence my boundaries or to place unrealistic expectations on me. What they portray as good, admirable, or successful often isn't.

God has a better plan for all of us. When we get our focus off the world and its standards, we can see how truly blessed we are—no matter what size we might be. "Therefore I tell you, do not worry about your life, what you will eat or drink; or about your body, what you will wear. Is not life more important than food, and the body more important than clothes?" (Matthew 6:25).

They Just Don't Understand: The Pressure of Parental Expectation

I totally get that you may feel as if your mom or dad don't understand what you're thinking or feeling. And if you are involved with a guy they don't like, I get that even more.

However, some people who seem like your enemies are really just good folks trying to do the best they know how to do. For the most part, they have enough love, common sense, compassion, and intelligence to differentiate right from wrong, good from bad, and healthy from unhealthy.

Yes, some parents may be better equipped than others psychologically and emotionally, and some may be healthier and more functional than others, but the majority want what is best for their kids. Your parents love you, even if some of them aren't always able to say it or show it in ways that make sense to you.

If your parents' expectations or actions are causing you stress, they might not realize it. Give them the benefit of the doubt and talk to them about it. The truth is, your parents are human beings, and it isn't always easy to juggle multiple responsibilities—trying to figure out how to balance their own "stuff" while helping you learn how to balance yours.

> Having a smart, gifted, talented, dramatic, passionate, and sometimes rebellious teenager takes a whole lot of energy.

If your parents nag, complain, scold, or demand that you change, try to understand where they are coming from. Having a smart, gifted, talented, dramatic, passionate, and sometimes rebellious teenager takes a whole lot of energy. Stop for a moment and put yourself in their shoes. These are some of the more challenging issues your parents may be dealing with as they care for you.

- trying to figure out how you think
- getting you to realize they are not the enemy
- dealing with the big and small problems of everyone in the household
- handling your challenging behavior
- addressing your negative thinking
- responding to your disrespectful attitudes
- conveying a sincere desire to establish wise and loving limits with realistic consequences
- worrying about your health and safety
- getting you to take responsibility for your actions
- getting you to understand they are not made of money
- trying to come up with the money to provide for your needs

- learning how to apply biblical principles to specific problems
- realizing the difference between helping and enabling you

The Expectations of Responsibility

I'm not going to tell you that everything the adults in your life are saying or doing is totally right, because I don't know that for certain. The fact is, some parents are coming from broken places. Some parents have struggled for years with their own issues, their own demons. Many parents who are less than perfect were themselves raised in a dysfunctional family. Might that be true of your parents?

It's reasonable for you to believe and trust that the people who are supposed to care for you are able to do just that. However, that may not always be the case. In the event this is true for you, a change in your expectations can change your life. Joyce Meyer addresses this topic.

> At age eighteen, we usually think we know everything, and certainly more than our parents and most adults we know. By age forty, we have realized we don't know much of anything and need all the wisdom we can get. At this point in life, we usually begin to gain some wisdom, much of which derives from the experiences we have had.
>
> The fact is, we learn much more about life from the things we go through than we ever do from books.
>
> We gain knowledge from books; we gain experience from life.
>
> Some teens do have more common sense than adults. Not all adults are doing what they should be doing in life. It seems almost everyone has personal problems, and I have observed that people with problems usually cause problems for those they are in relationship with.
>
> You as a teenager may be facing some difficult problems in your life right now. Those problems did not just appear suddenly; there is a reason, a root cause for them. But there is also a solution.[1]

Blaming your parents or anyone else is not the solution. And you can't always wear a convincing mask and meet unreasonable expectations. Going to school and pretending all day that everything is normal (if indeed it is not) is not the solution. That's no way to live.

The solution is to apply the "S" Step in SANITY and *Stop Ignoring Your Pain and Problems*. Take time to stop, step back, and pray about how other people's expectations might play a part in the exhaustion and stress you're feeling.

Ask the Holy Spirit to show you whether your expectations are reasonable, unreasonable, or simply different. Ask God for strength if your primary desire has been to fit in and not rock the boat, or if someone else's expectations are stressing you. Pray for wisdom and guidance about how you can set healthy boundaries and speak the truth in firmness and love in your relationships.

Focus on Your Job

Your job right now is not to get hung up on expectations, but to simply be a teenager—to let your body and brain grow in healthy ways and learn the skills that will enable you to function as an independent, contributing, and healthy adult. Your job is to learn how to handle yourself in situations of conflict and to set and maintain healthy boundaries in a way that honors God, the people you care about, and yourself. Your job is to work on strengthening your own identity, self-esteem, and self-respect so you can be the person God intended you to be—a powerful, precious, and purposeful daughter of the King.

Grab your notebook and write about areas in your life where expectations may be causing unhealthy, negative stress. And please be completely honest.

13

Violated Boundaries

Do you ever struggle with overwhelming stress and depression? Many young women do. When that happens, ask yourself whether any of your boundaries are being violated. If you're feeling confused or afraid because of all the pressure and stress you're experiencing, there's a good chance someone is crossing the line physically, verbally, emotionally, or sexually.

> When people violate the boundaries of your body or mind, they also violate your heart and soul.

When people violate the boundaries of your body or mind, they also violate your heart and soul. And when that happens, painful emotions and memories can continue to bubble beneath the surface for days, weeks, months, and in some cases for years—like lava waiting to erupt.

When your boundaries have been violated by others, either by force or by your own misunderstanding, ignorance, or fearful compliance, it can sometimes take years to learn how to rebuild them. Many young women who lack the love or attention of a father, who are looking for love in unhealthy ways, or who have been abused or molested are especially susceptible to boundary violations.

How Do We Know?

When we have weak or nonexistent personal boundaries, we can't always tell when someone has overstepped or violated them. In other words, if we don't know what our boundaries are, how do we know when someone has violated them?

Remember, if you truly want to cope with stress, you need to take a stand and set definitive standards for your life. You need to establish safe and acceptable boundaries for the way you allow people to treat you. You cannot change other people, but you can change the way you respond to them and to the way they treat you. Therefore, the stronger you become in defining your standards and understanding your boundaries, the easier it will be for you to know when someone is violating them and how to respond in a proactive and positive way.

Never feel that you have to apologize for having high standards, and don't ever lower your own standards to please someone else or because you are afraid of someone.

Boundary violations most often occur in a few key areas, and you can feel traumatic stress effects from one or more of these areas simultaneously.

- physical and emotional abuse
- sexual assault and pressure
- peer pressure and bullying (in person and online)
- Internet predators

No Time Limit

It's important to mention that while the stress effects of violated boundaries can often be felt immediately, they can also develop days, weeks, months, and even years after the actual incident. And as one boundary violation after another occurs, the emotional pressure can gradually build up and eventually cause a meltdown—like the one Missy experienced after years of pretending that everything was okay.

The Perfect Family

Once upon a time, a woman who worked as a church office manager was married to a man who was elected Sunday school superintendent in the same church. They were any pastor's dream couple—attractive, talented, relatively affluent, hardworking people who contributed to the weekly routine of church life.

But this couple had a secret. He was an abusive husband, she was a battered wife, and their daughter was caught in the cross fire.

The physical violence continued to escalate for years until the wife called the police, fearful that her husband was going to kill her. He had been pounding the back of her head into the kitchen cupboard, trying not to bruise her face. The pounding woke Missy, now a teenager, who came into the kitchen and witnessed the brutal attack. The mother managed to break free and call 911 just before she lost consciousness in Missy's arms. The husband was arrested and held for two days. When he was released, many people found it hard to believe that he was violent.

But not Missy. She always knew her father was a dangerous man. She knew her parents often fought, but she hid in her room and tried to pretend it wasn't happening.

Over the years, she had never questioned her mother's comments about being naturally clumsy or her frequent accidents. Missy's mother often had bruises on her arms, and the pain in her stomach, back, or ribs sometimes kept her in bed for days, wincing whenever she moved. Missy and her mother never discussed the incidents. They walked on eggshells in the aftermath of her father's rage.

Although his anger and violence were never directed at her, Missy grew up being emotionally abused by the constant lies, the pervasive fear, and the unquestioned control her father wielded over her fearful and compliant mother. Seeing the blood on her mother's body and the rage on her father's face that day when her mother called 911 deeply scarred Missy. The scars continued forming for years.

Fortunately, her mother finally applied the "A" step in SANITY— *Assemble Supportive People*—and reached out for professional intervention and help. This began a long journey to recovery that also included counseling for Missy, who began to exhibit symptoms of posttraumatic stress disorder (PTSD) shortly after witnessing the violent assault on her mother.

In counseling, Missy discovered that her psychological boundaries had been violated for years in the shadow of her parents' passive, aggressive, and violent lifestyle. She had learned by example to ignore pain, to deny problems, and to be meek, compliant, and fearful of saying no to anyone.

In fact, the truth quickly came out that Missy was being bullied at school and online. A couple of guys in one of her classes were pushing her around and teasing her. She had begun to cut that class to avoid them.

Missy never learned how to stand up for herself in a healthy way. As her parents' marriage fell apart, so did the facade of her pretend life.

> If your boundaries have been violated, you are already a survivor. You are *not* a victim.

The Courage to Be Strong

If your boundaries have been violated, you are already a survivor. You are *not* a victim. In fact, you must be a strong and courageous young woman to be willing to look at the role of violated boundaries in your life. I applaud you for the journey you are taking.

If you're asking questions and seeking answers, I'm confident you will find ways to set healthy boundaries and keep yourself going. You will learn the skills you need to protect and take care of yourself. There is a light at the end of what may seem like a very dark tunnel, and you *can* find hope and healing.

If you have been emotionally abused or have experienced sexual or physical abuse or threats, it's important for you to know that you're not alone. The next time you're in a room with four or more people, think about this.

- One in three teens experience sexual or physical abuse or threats from a boyfriend or girlfriend in one year.
- One in four women are sexually abused before the age of 18.
- One in four women experience violence from their partners in their lifetimes.

The Centers for Disease Control and Prevention report that every minute, 24 people in the United States are victims of rape, physical violence, or stalking by an intimate partner. Nearly one in four women around the globe are physically or sexually abused in their lifetimes, and gender violence kills and disables more women aged 15 to 44 than cancer, malaria, traffic accidents, or war.[1]

In a recent article in *Glamour Magazine*, Liz Brody wrote that over the course of an average year in twenty-first-century America, more than 1400 women will be murdered by someone they've loved.[2] That's more than four women killed *every single day* in the United States by someone they're involved with. And the rate of "intimate partner homicides" is climbing for young women who are in dating or cohabitation relationships.

Intimate partner homicide is a devastating result of relationship abuse—an aspect of domestic violence and one of the most extreme forms of violated boundaries. But did you know that domestic violence isn't just something that happens in a marriage gone bad? It happens in teenage relationships too.

Is it happening in yours?

What Is Domestic Violence?

Domestic violence is a pattern of behavior used to establish power and control over another person through fear and intimidation, often including the threat or use of violence. Here are some signs of an abusive relationship.

- exerting strict control (financial, social, or appearance)
- needing constant contact, including excessive texts and calls
- insulting a partner in front of other people
- extreme jealousy
- showing fear around a partner
- isolation from family and friends
- frequent canceling of plans at the last minute
- unexplained injuries or explanations that don't quite add up

What Is Sexual Assault?

Sexual assault is a crime motivated by a need to control, humiliate, and harm. Perpetrators use sexual assault as a weapon to hurt and dominate others. This occurs in more teenage relationships than adults are aware of or want to admit. Sexual assault is forced or coerced sexual contact without consent. *Consent is the presence of a clear yes, not the absence of a no.* It can take these forms:

- rape
- incest
- child sexual abuse and molestation
- oral sex
- harassment
- exposing and flashing
- forcing a person to pose for sexual pictures
- fondling or unwanted sexual touching above and under clothing
- force which may include but is not limited to...
  - use or display of a weapon
  - physical battering
  - immobilization of the victim

I know firsthand that violated boundaries *in all their forms* can cause long-lasting psychological and emotional effects, especially in young women. You may be feeling some of those effects in your life now.

Let's look at some of the effects when our boundaries are violated by abuse or sexual assault. Keep your journal nearby and write down any thoughts or feelings you may have as you read the descriptions to these eight effects.

- physical scars
- emotional scars
- depression
- isolation
- neglected appearance

- fear
- shame
- protective feelings

Physical Scars

Have you ever had bruises, stitches, or broken bones as a result of violence caused by someone else? Do you have visible scars or a permanent disability from any physical abuse? I know a young woman who was so badly raped that she will never be able to have children. The doctors said she was lucky to be alive, but for the longest time she didn't agree with them.

During my abusive teen marriage, my husband literally picked me up and threw me across the room. I landed on a metal milk crate and cut a huge gash in my right thigh that required many stitches. Although faint, the four-inch scar is still visible today, decades later. Additionally, the vision in my right eye was permanently impaired from another episode, and my bite has shifted over the years as a result of the empty socket where he knocked out two of my back teeth. My X-rays still bear witness to a half-dozen bone fractures on my ribs and arms.

No one ever laid a hand on me again in such a violent manner, but if I peer into the mirror and think real hard, I can remember how often I used to dab concealer on my black eyes and bruises. I can still recall the pain, confusion, fear, humiliation, and shame that accompanied episodes of violence. I can remember the elaborate lies I told the ER doctors or anyone who asked. And I can remember Jerry's lame excuses for hitting me and my lame excuses for accepting that treatment. Have you made up excuses like these?

"Oh, it's nothing, I'm just clumsy."

"I fell off my bike."

"It happened in gym class."

If you're making excuses to hide your abuse, it's time to apply the "N" step in SANITY and *Nip Excuses in the Bud*. Follow up immediately with the "A" step—*Assemble Supportive People*.

Violence is on the increase. Abusers have become much more savvy—they're careful not to hit above the neck, where clothing can't conceal the proof of their anger and rage. Please believe me—you *must* tell someone what is happening to you.

No more excuses about the physical scars. No more lies.

Your life may depend on it.

Emotional Scars

As painful as they can be, bruises will disappear in a matter of days or weeks. You can watch your skin change from purple to a mottled brownish yellow, and eventually the discoloration will no longer be visible. However, the emotional scars of abuse are invisible, and their effects can last far longer. When your boundaries are violated, a part of your heart, soul, and mind is forever changed. How you view the world is forever changed. How you view yourself is never the same.

Missy spent years living under the cloud of her father's violent nature and her mother's passive denial, and that shaped how she felt about herself, her parents, marriage, conflict, and relationships in general. She carried the emotional scars of posttraumatic stress, and she will tell you today that professional counseling saved her sanity—and her life.

This is where it is critical to apply the "A" step in SANITY. You must begin to *Assemble Supportive People* around you. Go back and review this vital "A" step in chapter 10. Then pray about your next step. Ask God to shine light on the steps He wants you to take.

And always remember that you are *never* alone.

Depression

Statistics show that up to 20 percent of girls aged 10 to 19 are experiencing episodes of major depression, including withdrawal, tearfulness, repeated negative thoughts, sleep disturbance, self-destructive acts, and even suicide. If you never seem to have any energy and you're tired all the time, if your emotions are all over the charts, or if you're fearful of thinking about your future, you may be suffering from depression.

Do you think of yourself and your life as worthless? Do you sleep too much or too little? Has your eating changed, or have you gained or lost weight without wanting to? Do you think about dying or killing yourself?

If so, it's time to apply the "S" step and *Stop Ignoring Your Pain and Problems.*

Isolation

An abuser is likely to gain control by keeping you separated from people close to you. Has your boyfriend demanded that you spend less time with your friends and family? Have you started to withdraw from people for any of these reasons?

- You're afraid people will know you're being mistreated or abused.
- They already know, and now you feel ashamed and humiliated.
- People might think you caused this.
- They won't understand how you got involved in the situation.
- You think nobody will believe you.

The answer is not to withdraw from society, from your existence, or from your identity. The answer is to consistently apply *all* of the SANITY Steps and to refuse to be isolated. Healthy relationships don't put you in a cocoon—they empower you to soar!

Neglected Appearance

If you have been physically or sexually abused, molested, or threatened, you may find yourself dressing in baggy and unattractive clothing to avoid triggering more abuse. Sometimes we grow to hate ourselves and our own bodies. Have you gained or lost a lot of weight because you don't want guys to look at you? Have you stopped wearing makeup, styling your hair, or doing your nails? Are you afraid to look attractive?

Suddenly neglecting your appearance is a sign of a deeper problem. If you dig deeper, you'll eventually identify the pain. When you expose it, it will lose its power over you. It's time to stop ignoring the pain.

Fear

Do loud noises make you jump? Do you feel anxiety when you're in a crowd? Does your stomach ache when you hear somebody arguing, or do you panic when you see someone who reminds you of your abuser? Are you terrified of making mistakes or saying the wrong thing, no matter who you're with? Do you have nightmares or flashbacks about the violence you suffered? Are you afraid this person is going to try to hurt you again? Has someone threatened you in the past, or is this person still threatening or harassing you?

Fear can cause you to make choices and respond to people and situations in unhealthy and dangerous ways. Stress is often caused by fear, and fear follows most traumatic experiences. So it's important to delve deeper into your feelings to see what might be causing your fear.

It's pretty hard to do that on your own as a young woman. Reach out to someone and tell them you are afraid.

Shame

Shame is always a negative emotion. It combines feelings of unworthiness, embarrassment, and dishonor. As a child, I thought something was terribly wrong with me because of my debilitating fear of the dark and my nightmares. I also knew something was wrong because of the way my mind worked. It quickly jumped from one thought to the next, and the way I saw numbers and letters was different from the way my classmates did. I felt like a freak and an embarrassment to my mother.

When Jerry hit me, I sometimes blamed myself. I felt as if there was so much wrong with me, I deserved to be treated poorly. And when I was finally able to escape that relationship, I felt ashamed that I had stayed in it for so long—that I had allowed myself to be treated in such a horrible way. I was ashamed of who I was, what I did and didn't do, and even what others did to me.

It was an awful way to live. To this day, I am my own worst enemy as I struggle with negative feelings and tend to blame myself for things that are not my fault.

When we carry unwarranted shame, we bottle things up so much that we suffocate our identity. Shame is one of the most powerful and distorted feelings that Satan uses to keep us from being effective women and from walking in victory.

Protective Feelings

Do you protect the person who has violated your boundaries? If a boyfriend has hit you, a family member has molested you, a classmate has threatened you, or someone close has raped you, are you protecting this person because you're afraid of them—or afraid of what might happen if you tell someone the truth? Do you protect your abuser so the truth won't get out? Are you afraid to trust anyone?

Setting boundaries is a healthy way to protect yourself, but building a wall of protective feelings around the effects of abuse or around an abuser is *never* healthy.

How to Get Help

Remember, you can begin to accumulate unnecessary emotional baggage as a teen that will only grow heavier every year and greatly affect your life as an adult. Or you can address it *now* and be free.

I never reached out for help when I was a teenager. I didn't think I could—or should. I couldn't go online for information or help. I couldn't call a hotline or text an advocate because none of those resources existed. I felt completely alone. And those feelings didn't stop even after I escaped the abuse. I felt my only option was to keep a stiff upper lip, accept responsibility for my life and the life of my son, and just keep on keeping on.

I never addressed the reasons why my search for love was so misguided. I never got help to learn healthy coping skills or conflict resolution. I never asked anyone how to address our basic needs—to feel safe, protected, valued, and nurtured. I never exposed my pain or confronted my problems in a way that would allow me to heal and become whole emotionally, psychologically, and spiritually.

Instead, I spent years running like a crazy person on the gerbil wheel of insanity, reacting emotionally instead of responding rationally, overwhelmed by feelings of shame, guilt, anger, and fear.

I kept putting temporary Band-Aids on my horribly wounded heart when what I needed was professional help and guidance to sort out my thoughts and emotions. More important, I needed to learn my true value and identity, how to make decisions based on rational thought and not on emotional feeling, and how to set healthy boundaries with firmness and love.

I was in my early twenties the first time I talked with a professional therapist about the physical abuse I experienced as a teenager. I wanted to find the strength to approach my mother and ask for the truth about what had happened to me as a toddler in that temporary foster home. Sadly, I only scratched the surface of self-discovery before I decided I was healed. Frankly, the pain of dealing with the pain was too much to handle. Especially for someone without faith.

I was in my midthirties when I finally embraced God as my heavenly Father and the Lord Jesus Christ as my Savior. Barely a year later, I had an emotional breakdown that sent me into a 30-day residential treatment program, and I finally began to undo the damage caused by years of ignoring my pain and problems.

> Don't let the emotional baggage you are beginning to carry now become a freight load of regret you'll carry later.

Don't wait as long as I did to make sense of the pain and confusion you are feeling now. If your boundaries have been violated, tell someone the truth. Apply the "A" step in SANITY and begin now to *Assemble Supportive People* who can help you. Don't let the emotional baggage you are beginning to carry now become a freight load of regret you'll carry later.

And you can start with these valuable resources.

- Call the 24-hour National Domestic Violence Hotline at 1-800-799-SAFE (7233) or TTY 1-800-787-3224 or visit their website at www.thehotline.org.

- Call LoveIsRespect.org at 1-866-331-9474 or text "loveis" to 77054 or live chat at www.loveisrespect.org.

- And if you are dealing with rape, abuse, or incest, you can find hope in the RAINN—the Rape, Abuse, Incest National Network. Call 1-800-656-HOPE (4673).

Leaving the Past Behind

God knows what you have been through. He knows your pain and the secrets you carry in your heart. And He wants you to be free from the bondage of every boundary violation you have ever experienced.

There is a story in the fourth chapter of the book of John in the Bible about a woman whose heart was broken from years of violated boundaries.

Tired from a long walk, Jesus sat wearily beside a well. When a Samaritan woman appeared at the well in the heat of the day, Jesus asked her for a drink of water. In the desert, no one went to the well in the middle of the day—especially not at high noon. Clearly this woman deliberately timed her visit. She chose to come to the well when she knew no one else would be there, when she could avoid stares of condemnation and whispers behind her back. She had apparently made quite a name for herself in her pursuit of love, and it wasn't a good one. She must have had something going for her, something that would attract men—looks, charm, that certain something. Yet we learn through this story that none of her relationships lasted.

The Bible doesn't tell us anything about the life this woman lived with her previous husbands—only that she was on number six and wasn't actually married to him at all. One can only surmise that her heart had been broken more than once. And it's a strong possibility her first heartbreak was as a teenager. She may well have suffered abuse and violated boundaries at some point in her life. As a result, this woman probably carried a great many painful secrets in her heart.

It breaks my own heart to envision her alone, subjecting herself to the sweltering heat to avoid disparaging attitudes and comments. Burying the pain of abuse, fear, shame, and poor choices, she probably felt far older than her years.

Yet it was by divine plan that she met Jesus at the well that day.

Jesus exposed her secrets, offering her living water and truth. He set her free from the pain and the stress she felt because of her past.

"The woman left her water jar beside the well and ran back to the village, telling everyone" (John 4:28 NLT). I'd like to believe she left more than the jar behind.

She would never be the same.

I left my own jar of secrets by the well when Jesus Christ took my broken spirit and lost soul, turned me around, and set me on a new course. He began to heal the pain of my violated boundaries and fill that empty place in my soul I had been so desperately trying to fill with food, drugs, relationships, material goods, work, and empty pursuits. He forgave me the sins that weighed heavy on my heart, showing me I no longer had to carry that burden.

He led me to a group of professional counselors who held my hands and heart through an intensive season of healing. Over the years He has blessed me with individuals, support groups, and wise Christian friends who have continued to help me get through tough times.

He can do the same for you. God knows exactly what you need when you need it.

Tell Somebody

The key factor in coping with symptoms of stress caused by violence is to expose your secrets to the light of day. Don't let them fester inside your heart and infect your spirit and soul. Tell somebody.

Reach out to someone on a crisis hotline or to a Christian counselor, pastor, friend, loved one, or support group member. Just tell somebody.

If you are currently being physically, emotionally, or sexually abused in any kind of relationship, don't wait—tell somebody.

If something traumatic happened to you in the past—even if it was a long time ago—tell somebody.

Perhaps you are an abuser yourself and you truly desire to change your behavior. When you feel angry, do not hit somebody—tell somebody.

If you suspect someone is being physically abused, say something to them. Even an awkward, uncomfortable conversation is better than saying nothing. Still, the person getting hurt has to be the one to decide to do something about it. It is *their* responsibility to tell somebody. If you are a friend or family member of someone who is being abused, it's important for you to support her and help her find a way to safety and peace. But be very careful about trying to rescue your friend or loved one.

The National Domestic Violence Hotline has posted a very helpful article about how you can help someone who is being abused. It's called "How can you help a friend or family member?" Check it out at www.the hotline.org/help/help-for-friends-and-family/.

Running Away Is Not an Option

There is no doubt in my mind that God was watching out for me when I ran away from home when I was 14. However, that was in 1970, and the world is a much different place now. If violated boundaries have caused overwhelming stress in your life and you are considering the possibility of running away from home, I beg you to look at other alternatives and consider the hard reality of what could happen to you.

One in eight endangered runaways reported to the National Center for Missing and Exploited Children in 2012 were most likely sex trafficking victims.[3] This means they were lured into the dark and dangerous world of prostitution, pornography, and drugs against their will. They were likely imprisoned, abused, and sold as property.

In June 2003, the FBI, the Department of Justice Child Exploitation and Obscenity Section, and the National Center for Missing and Exploited Children launched the Innocence Lost National Initiative. Their combined efforts were aimed at addressing the growing problem of domestic sex trafficking of children and adolescents in the United States.

These groups have successfully rescued more than 2700 children. Investigations have successfully led to the conviction of more than 1300 individuals who exploit children through prostitution.[4]

Unfortunately, this is a very real danger. In fact, many of these confused, lonely, and frightened young girls were introduced to their abusers and captors while in the comfort of their own homes—online. Make sure to read the short but powerful chapter 14, "Internet Predators and Cyberbullies." And no matter how awful your situation is, *don't run away.*

Looking for Love

During my teen years, the longing to hear "I love you" drew me toward people who didn't know the true meaning of love any more than I did. Having no loving father, struggling with learning disabilities, suffering early childhood abuse, having nightmares and being afraid of the dark…these set the stage for many of the poor choices I would make as a teen and later as an adult. Considering all I had experienced, it made perfect sense that I would have trouble understanding and setting healthy boundaries. No wonder I fell victim as a teen to someone who brutally violated them. I wanted desperately to fill the empty place in my heart and soul.

If you're trying to make sense of the pain and confusion of traumatic abuse in your life, I encourage you to read two powerful books by one amazing author—*The Wall Around Your Heart: How Jesus Heals You When Others Hurt You* and the e-book *Not Marked: Finding Hope and Healing After Sexual Abuse*. Mary DeMuth has written these books for adults, and they contain some graphic descriptions, so please ask your parents' permission to read them.

I believe with all my heart that God is using Mary's voice to open doors to hope and healing for those of us who have been deeply hurt by abuse and are struggling to understand why. Mary has lived a profoundly painful life, but she has found incredible healing and unconditional love in the arms of Jesus. Here is part of her story.

> After a traumatic childhood, where God's name was a swear word, and my pleas to go to Sunday school were ignored, I had no idea how to begin with Jesus. I honestly didn't know He existed.
>
> What I did know: something about me felt fundamentally broken. I had no safe place to talk through the devastation of my childhood, no one to tell about childhood rape at five or talk through my father's death when I was ten. More than that, I believed I was a walking mistake, a fluke of a girl who shouldn't have been born, meant to be in the way—a nuisance. I didn't experience fond affection or nurturing. In almost every way, I lived alone, unable to rightly process the pain that others had inflicted my way. Had I never met Jesus, I'd have spent my entire life in reverse, reliving the aftermath year after year, learning clever ways to numb my pain, excite my life, or end it all.
>
> In the eighth grade, the past caught up with me. I was a combustive mess, a volatile cocktail of unmet expectations, loneliness, anger, and fear. The actions of others piled on top of me, and I couldn't find hope in that darkness. I wanted to end my life.

Chances are, you've been in a place like that once or twice, where other people's actions have hijacked you. You're like Joseph from the book of Genesis whose brothers sold him into slavery. Through no fault of your own, you scratch around in an earthen pit, longing for rescue, only to be enslaved the moment someone pulls you from the hole. This is how people's lives venture into pain's path. They find short rescue only to live a lifetime enslaved to that pain.

I could not see out of the pit at fourteen years old. I didn't want to see out of it. I'd resigned myself to a sad life or no life at all.[5]

Just Say No to the Lie

Many young girls today are conditioned to ignore their pain and problems. They have resigned themselves to the lie that stress is a part of living in our culture and that they just have to deal with it.

Not true.

If violated boundaries are linked to your stress, you may need help to do some deep introspection and address these significant and painful life issues at the core of your being—issues that could include childhood abuse or molestation, depression, domestic violence, divorce, parental abandonment, rape, alcoholism, addictions, and bipolar disorders to name a few.

Please don't hesitate to get the help you need.

However, if you begin to reach out for help using online resources, be responsible and exercise caution. The Internet is an amazing place, but it can pose a threat to your safety if you aren't aware of the potential hazards.

Danger is real, but fear is a choice. Don't be afraid to reach out—just be careful.

14

Internet Predators and Cyberbullies

Adolescence is a challenging time in the best of circumstances, but it's infinitely harder if you're trying to cope with stress or when your boundaries have been violated in any way. It makes sense that you are looking for someone to understand what you're going through. Just be very careful when it comes to online communication.

It's important for you to know that online sex offenders can be any age or sex. They often don't fit the stereotype of a dirty, unkempt, older man wearing a raincoat. But they can harm you. Take a few minutes to read this very scary FBI information.

> It makes sense that you are looking for someone to understand what you're going through. Just be very careful when it comes to online communication.

While online computer exploration opens a world of possibilities for young people, expanding their horizons and exposing them to different cultures and ways of life, they can be exposed to dangers as they hit the road exploring the information highway. There are individuals who attempt to sexually exploit children through the use of online services and the Internet.

Some of these individuals gradually seduce their targets through the use of attention, affection, kindness, and even gifts. These individuals are often willing to devote considerable amounts of time, money, and energy in this process. They listen to and empathize with the problems of children. They will be aware of the latest music, hobbies, and interests of children. These individuals attempt to gradually lower children's inhibitions by slowly introducing sexual context and content into their conversations.

There are other individuals, however, who immediately engage in sexually explicit conversation with children. Some offenders primarily collect and trade child-pornographic images, while others seek face-to-face meetings with children via online contacts. It is important for parents to understand that children can be indirectly victimized through conversation, i.e. "chat," as well as the transfer of sexually explicit information and material. Computer-sex offenders may also be evaluating children they come in contact with online for future face-to-face contact and direct victimization.

Children, especially adolescents, are sometimes interested in and curious about sexuality and sexually explicit material. They may be moving away from the total control of parents and seeking to establish new relationships outside their family. Because they may be curious, children/adolescents sometimes use their online access to actively seek out such materials and individuals. Sex offenders targeting children will use and exploit these characteristics and needs. Some adolescent children may also be attracted to and lured by online offenders closer to their age who, although not technically child molesters, may be dangerous. Nevertheless, they have been seduced and manipulated by a clever offender and do not fully understand or recognize the potential danger of these contacts.[1]

Cyberbullies

Unfortunately, strangers aren't the only ones who can hurt you with Internet technology. The huge rise in social networking has opened doors for mean girls and guys to wreak emotional havoc and conduct character assassination on a massive scale.

"Cyberbullying" is defined as a person tormenting, threatening, harassing, or embarrassing another person using the Internet or other technologies, such as cell phones. It has become a global problem.

> With the explosion in use of online communication tools, it is no surprise that some kids decided to misuse the technology to be malicious or menacing towards others. The fact that teens are connected to technology 24/7 means that they are susceptible to victimization (as well as become bullies towards others) around the clock. Apart from a measure of anonymity, it is easier to be hateful when using typed words rather than spoken words. And because some adults have been slow to respond to cyberbullying, many cyberbullies feel that there are little to no consequences to their actions.
>
> Cyberbullying crosses all geographic boundaries with the spread of the Internet. The spread of the Internet was to have a positive impact on the world, so more people can stay connected and life could be easier. But some kids feel free to post or send whatever they want while online without considering the effects it may have on the other person, his/her family and his/her friends.[2]

The psychological and emotional outcomes of cyberbullying are similar to those of face-to-face bullying. The difference is, in-person bullying often ends when school ends. There is no escape from cyberbullying. Violated boundaries through online attacks are significantly damaging and ruining young lives. And it's getting worse.

1. Nearly 43% of kids have been bullied online. 1 in 4 has had it happen more than once.

2. 70% of students report seeing frequent bullying online.

3. Over 80% of teens use a cell phone regularly, making it the most common medium for cyber bullying.

4. 68% of teens agree that cyber bullying is a serious problem.

5. 81% of young people think bullying online is easier to get away with than bullying in person.

6. 90% of teens who have seen social-media bullying say they have ignored it. 84% have seen others tell cyber bullies to stop.

7. Only 1 in 10 victims will inform a parent or trusted adult of their abuse.

8. Girls are about twice as likely as boys to be victims and perpetrators of cyber bullying.

9. About 58% of kids admit someone has said mean or hurtful things to them online. More than 4 out 10 say it has happened more than once.

10. About 75% have visited a website bashing another student.

11. Bullying victims are 2 to 9 times more likely to consider committing suicide.[3]

It's important to be aware of the statistics, but it's even more critical for you to be aware of the consequences. If you send mean words and vicious gossip, the damage you are doing could be life-threatening and potentially illegal. This isn't a game.

If you are on the receiving end of someone's cruelty, anger, or ignorance, it is vital that you remember what we've talked about in previous chapters. You will have more power and better results when you can approach any form of cyberbullying with *rational thinking* and not *emotional responding*. This is particularly true when it comes to this form of assault—and it *is* assault.

In the event you read something negative online about you or someone you care about, do not lower yourself to the level of a cyberbully. Apply the "S" Step immediately and *Stop* everything! Resist the immediate urge to defend or explain yourself. Don't respond to the assaulting post, text, e-mail, or website until you've taken time to think it through—and only after you seek the advice and counsel of someone older and wiser.

Remember, your words are just as powerful as those of your attacker, and they, too, can exist forever in cyberspace. Let your good words recirculate, not the negative ones you may regurgitate in a weak moment of emotional reaction and pain.

Get Help Today

There are literally hundreds of online sources where you can learn how to avoid and stop Internet predators and get help for cyberbullying issues. Ask God to direct your course of action and to open doors to get the help you need to address your particular situation and to **stop** ignoring the pain. Here are a couple of organizations you can start with.

- Enough Is Enough—Making the Internet Safe for Children and Families (InternetSafety101.org)
- End to Cyber Bullying Organization (EndCyberBullying.org)

Many young women who are bullied in person or online have also resigned themselves to being controlled by angry, jealous, and violent boyfriends. These girls are victims of dating violence. In some cases they don't even recognize that they are being abused or that their boundaries have been violated by the guys in their lives.

Are you one of these girls?

15

Teen Dating Violence

Many young girls are so hungry to love and be loved that they endure unacceptable treatment at the hands of their boyfriends or a series of boyfriends.

A pattern of involvement in unhealthy relationships can start early and last a lifetime. Dating violence often starts with teasing and name calling. These behaviors are often thought to be normal parts of a relationship. But they can set the stage for more serious violence, such as physical assault and rape.

Unfortunately, our world has become increasingly violent, and many people are angry, confused, and lashing out in irrational ways. Kyle Hargrove, a licensed Christian counselor, told me he is seeing a marked increase in boundary violations among teenagers.

> My colleagues and I are finding that more and more young men are becoming increasingly violent and controlling. They are angry, and rightfully so in many instances. However, they are directing their anger toward young women who are, in turn, becoming increasingly fearful, compliant, and victimized.

Teen dating violence includes any physical, sexual, psychological, and emotional violence in a dating relationship, as well as stalking. It can occur in person or electronically by a current or former dating partner. You may have heard several different words used to describe teen dating violence. Here are just a few.

- relationship abuse
- intimate partner violence
- relationship violence
- dating abuse
- domestic abuse
- domestic violence

A 2011 Youth Risk Behavior Survey by the Centers for Disease Control and Prevention included these statistics.

> Adolescents and adults are often unaware that teens experience dating violence. In a nationwide survey, 9.4 percent of high school students report being hit, slapped, or physically hurt on purpose by their boyfriend or girlfriend in the 12 months prior to the survey. About 1 in 5 women and nearly 1 in 7 men who ever experienced rape, physical violence, and/or stalking by an intimate partner, first experienced some form of partner violence between 11 and 17 years of age.[1]

Did you get that? One in five women who have experienced rape, physical violence, or stalking first experienced some form of partner violence between 11 and 17 years of age!

How old are you? How old are most of your friends?

No one is immune to facing conflict. There will always be some level of drama, chaos, and crisis to deal with in life—often in the form of a challenging person or situation that will test your patience and try your nerves. The question is, how will you respond to conflict when people overstep their boundaries?

Looking for Love in All the Wrong Places

When Jerry began physically abusing me, he was careful not to leave evidence for anyone to see. He grabbed my arms and wrists, or he punched and kicked me in my stomach and ribs. I never fought back, and I was too afraid and ashamed to tell anyone. And his remorse afterward seemed sincere, especially when he cried and begged me to forgive him, swearing that it would never happen again. But it did happen again. And again. It didn't take long before he didn't seem to care where he hit me, and black eyes, split lips, and facial bruises were frequent. After a while, the number of visible scars on my body increased like a roadmap of violence stretching across my skin. Yet that paled in comparison to what was happening in my heart and soul.

> Just because you don't talk about bad things doesn't mean their effects automatically disappear. That's not how it works.

I was only 15, but I felt decades older.

Back then, there were no shelters for battered women, no easily accessible counseling centers, no safe places, no hotlines, and no rape crisis centers. I was 16 when I discovered I was pregnant and feared for the life of my unborn child. There was nowhere for me to go except back home—to the place where no one talked about their feelings, where emotions were buried and healthy conflict resolution was unheard of.

I was thankful that my mother welcomed me with open arms, and I'm not sure what would have happened otherwise. But burying the emotional burden of abuse and ignoring pain is never healthy. Just because you don't talk about bad things doesn't mean their effects automatically disappear. That's not how it works.

When I gave birth to my son, got my GED, and started vocational training at the local beauty school, no one advised or counseled me, no one spoke into my life with wisdom or guidance, no one told me that there was more to being a parent than accepting responsibility and declaring undying love for my child. Nobody told me it was possible for me to make a U-turn with my life and find the happiness that seemed so out of reach.

It was a full five years later that we moved across the country and I was finally able to escape the ever-present fear and threat of violence from my ex-husband. However, the damage was already done. Unfortunately, the unresolved and unexamined pain of my teen years was the foundation on which decades of shattered dreams, broken promises, and poor choices would be built.

The Pain of Denial

Here's a typical scenario of teen dating violence.

> A boyfriend uses verbal attacks and humiliation to stay in con-
> trol of his girlfriend. He constantly criticizes her, making her
> feel bad about herself. He's possessive and jealous, calling or
> texting her all the time to make sure where she is and to accuse
> her of being with other guys. He knows exactly how to hurt
> her and so she is watchful, afraid to upset him. She apologizes
> all the time. She is aware that she can't do anything separate
> from him and so she stops spending time with her best friend.
> The emotional abuse begins to escalate to physical. If he has
> convinced her to have sex, what may have once seemed spe-
> cial has become rough. He uses or threatens to use physical
> force. He's pushed her against the lockers at school. Now he's
> hit her a couple of times. And she can't stand the thought of
> losing him.[2]

When you find yourself attracted to a really cute guy and then realize
that he is attracted to you too, your inner voice is not likely to be saying,
Make sure this is a healthy relationship. At that moment, all you want is to
be in that relationship—to be half of a couple and blissfully in love. And
if you're looking at this really cute guy to fill any kind of emptiness in your
heart or to help you escape from something painful in your life, you're
also not likely to recognize (or admit) the warning signs that accompany
an unhealthy relationship. Suddenly, you find yourself ignoring or excus-
ing dangerous behavior. You get caught up in a whirlwind of emotions.

What happens to a young woman's heart when someone she loves
becomes the cause of her pain and the object of her anguish? How does
she reconcile her feelings of love, confusion, and fear?

Here are a few of the many reasons why some guys result to violence
in their relationships with girls.

- jealousy
- using violence to assert power
- lack of respect for women
- violence during his childhood

- unresolved insecurity and anger
- alcohol and drug use

Several excellent resources are available to help you delve deeper into this issue. I highly recommend two books written by author and therapist Barrie Levy—*In Love and in Danger: A Teen's Guide to Breaking Free of Abusive Relationships* and *Dating Violence: Young Women in Danger.* These are both older books, but they're still available online. Here's a sample of how this insightful author helps teen girls to better understand what's going on with violent guys.

> Young men often believe it is their right to abuse a woman. They may mistakenly believe that men should dominate and control women, and that women are passive, stupid and obligated to please men.
>
> There is a lot of peer pressure on guys to be sexually active, so sometimes they are sexually aggressive with girls. Guys feel it is their role to be dominant and to control their girlfriends' activities and behavior.
>
> Guys get approval from their friends for being "the boss," for keeping their girlfriend "in line" by pushing her around, or for ignoring her when she says no to sex. They may be afraid they won't look "man enough" if they don't behave this way.[3]

If your boyfriend wants to get help and change his behavior, he needs to discover the reasons why he becomes violent. However, if you are being abused in any way, it's far more important for you to know why you think and feel that you deserve to be abused. Where is your self-worth, self-respect, and identity? You may find yourself wondering, *If he loves me, why does he hurt me?* But maybe that's the wrong question. Instead, ask yourself, *Why do I stay in this relationship and allow him to hurt me?*

Barrie Levy says girls stay in abusive relationship for various reasons.

> Girls feel pressured to do what their boyfriends want them to do, even if it hurts them. Girls often learn to be dependent on their boyfriends. They learn to put him first, and not have anything in their lives apart from the relationship. They are

judgmental and critical of girls who are not seeing one special guy. A girl feels peer pressure to be in a relationship, even if it is not good for her.

Girls feel pressured to have sex when they don't want to. A girl may blame herself if her boyfriend makes her have sex in spite of her saying no. The pressure comes from mistaken ideas about sex and about relationships. For example, teenagers often believe that if a guy takes a girl out, she is "obligated" to have sex with him, even if she doesn't want to. Many teenagers believe that guys are justified in raping a girl if they are turned on by her or if they have spent money on her. Once a girl agrees to have sex with her boyfriend, she may believe that she doesn't have the right to say no, or to change her mind or not want to do particular sex acts, or she may believe she doesn't have the right to say no on another date—as if he "owns" her. Or she may be afraid that she will lose her "reputation" if she doesn't agree to his "ownership" of her.

These beliefs contribute to dating violence.[4]

Stand Up and Stand Strong

As a teen, you begin to cultivate an increasing awareness of the world that exists outside of your own world. Sometimes that alternative world appears far more attractive than your own, especially when you have experienced intense pain and loss and want nothing more than to distance yourself from the world you grew up in.

For example, if you have been neglected or abused in any way as a child, you may find yourself gravitating to anyone who shows an interest in you, regardless of his lifestyle or behavior. That can be very dangerous. Likewise, if you have been overly protected and sheltered, you may find yourself trusting people who have not earned your trust. In both instances, it's important to use good judgment. Some guys can love, respect, and care for you in healthy ways. But other guys prey on emotional vulnerability— they thrive on it—and those guys can be very dangerous.

Sometimes, we are blinded by love and attention.

That's why it's important for you to respect and adhere to the "boyfriend boundaries" your parents may have established for you—even if you don't always agree with them. In most cases, their age gives them the wisdom and ability to judge upright character and emotional authenticity. If your parents have set boundaries for you, you're several positive steps ahead of some of your friends whose parents are totally clueless about the need to set reasonable boundaries for their daughters. And if you're realizing that your parents have neglected to set appropriate boundaries for you, it's all the more reason to incorporate the SANITY steps into your life on your own.

My mother could see the kind of person Jerry was from the start. She saw his character, she could tell he was unethical and false, and she could sense he was dangerous. But I wouldn't listen. I thought I knew better than she did.

I was so wrong.

Give yourself time to learn how to accurately judge someone's character. If someone's actions don't match his words, he's revealing his poor character. Set your standards high and include a zero tolerance for physical, verbal, or emotional abuse. And remember, dating is *not* the same as being married, regardless of what some guys might say.

> There's a big difference between *feeling* grown-up and *being* grown-up.

And one more thing. No matter how grown-up you may feel, you are still a teenager, and you're still developing in many ways. There's a big difference between *feeling* grown-up and *being* grown-up.

What Do You Think?

You've just read back-to-back chapters on violated boundaries and violence in teen dating relationships. While your thoughts are fresh, grab your journal and put today's date and the suggested header at the top of the page (see below), and then answer the three questions. But first, take a moment to recite the short prayer below. It's important to ask God for direction in just about everything you do in life, and developing the habit of intentional prayer is one of the smartest choices you can make to conquer stress.

Dear Lord,

This is a very difficult and painful subject. Please open my eyes and heart to know what You want me to do. Show me the course of action You want me to take. Give me the strength and courage to help myself or someone else to expose the pain and confront the problem of relationship abuse and violated boundaries. Help me to keep You at the center of my life and to understand my identity in You. Help me to set my standards, feel secure in my self-worth, and acquire the skills I need to set and maintain healthy boundaries in all areas of my life.

I love You, Lord, and I know that You love me too. I know You don't want me to deal with this on my own, so please help me reach out to someone who can be supportive in a healthy way.

Amen.

Date:_____

What I Think About Violated Boundaries and Relationship Abuse

1. Has this topic touched you personally? If so, how?

2. What do you know now about this topic that you didn't know before you read these chapters?

3. What do you feel God is telling you to do concerning this topic?

16

Life Interrupted— a Baby Changes Everything

Maternal instincts are strong no matter how young you are. However, getting pregnant doesn't mean that you are magically gifted with the necessary knowledge, wisdom, and physical energy for motherhood.

"Baby mama" has emerged as a demeaning tag for a woman who has a child when she isn't married and when her relationship with the father is mostly about sex. Being a baby mama is not the same as being a responsible mother. (The same can be said about being a baby daddy—it's quite different from being a responsible father.)

> When we have weak or nonexistent boundaries, we can give ourselves away to a guy who convinces us that he's our knight in shining armor.

Sadly, today's culture teaches us that intimacy before marriage is acceptable. Yet that is not how God wants us to live. When we have weak or nonexistent boundaries, we can give ourselves away to a guy who convinces us that he's our knight in shining armor. Unfortunately, that rarely turns out to be the case. However, it's important to know that God will love us unconditionally, even if a relationship doesn't turn out as we expected and even if we become pregnant.

Biblical Standards for Parenthood

The standards God sets for us as His children are good and just. So are the standards God sets for us as parents of our own children. Remember Proverbs 22:6? "Start children off on the way they should go, and even when they are old they will not turn from it."

> It can be more than a bit challenging when a person with low self-esteem and self-worth is responsible for pouring healthy attributes into a child…

As a teen mom, I loved my son more than my own life. That might sound good at first, but in reality it was unhealthy and unbalanced. It can be more than a bit challenging when a person with low self-esteem and self-worth is responsible for pouring healthy attributes into a child—no matter how good her intentions may be.

Yes, my intentions were good, but my skewed standards were more than a bit off base. Back then, I didn't believe in God, and I raised my son by a mishmash of standards I culled from what I had learned in my own dysfunctional childhood, what I saw on television and in the movies, and what I gleaned from studying Eastern religions and New Age spirituality. Other than my distorted sense of responsibility and control, I provided very little consistency and almost no emotional integrity in my son's life.

My own life spiraled out of control during my son's formative years, and it makes perfect sense to me now that he would turn to drugs and start running away from home when he was 13. But at the time it was confusing, devastating, and frightening.

I tried so hard to be a good mom, but in my confused and young mind, my idea of a "good mom" was often quite different from God's standard. After all these years, it's hard to say how things would have been different if I had made smarter choices as a teen mom. But I have to believe the years would have been filled with much less drama if I had placed God at the center of my life when I decided to be a mother.

Life-Changing News

I discovered I was pregnant during a visit to a hospital emergency room, where I was getting stitches in my leg. I can't recall the lie I told on that visit to explain my injury, but I can vividly recall that my husband's violence landed me there. I was 15 years old, and we had been married for seven months.

The physical abuse started on our wedding day. We were in the car leaving the courthouse in Greenville, South Carolina, and I said something to Jerry about getting something to eat. He reached across the front seat and slapped me across the face—hard.

I was stunned.

His apology was convincing, and thus began the vicious cycle of his being romantic, passionate, explosive, violent, and apologetic—a prime example of gerbil-wheel insanity.

Instead of living the fairy-tale dream I envisioned, the months following our wedding became a nightmare, and the periods of calm between the storms of violence grew shorter and shorter. I became certain he would kill me, but I always believed his promises to change. It was as if I was addicted to the sick and dangerous love we shared.

When the ER doctor told me I was about two months pregnant, I was overcome with the weight of my responsibility for my child's life. I was so broken and damaged, I didn't have the strength or confidence to get out of the abusive relationship in order to save my own life. But I reached deep down and found it when I realized I was responsible for the life of another human being. In essence, my child's life saved my own.

When my son was born, I was living with my mother, going through a divorce, and trying desperately to survive while being stalked and threatened by my volatile soon-to-be ex-husband. I was 16 years old and ill prepared for the enormous responsibility of motherhood.

You don't have to be as uninformed as I was if you discover you're pregnant. During my research for this book, I came across a website for Christian teens. It's called, *Fervr: Daily Articles, Reviews & Videos for Christian Teens.* You can find it at Fervr.net

Fervr had a blurb for a book filled with insight. I wish I'd had it as a pregnant teen. It's called *A Life Already Started: Finding a Positive Path in Unplanned Pregnancy* by Dr. Megan Best. Here's what Fervr.net has to say about this important book.

> Pregnant?
> Don't panic. You're not alone.
>
> When you are faced with an unwanted pregnancy, it may feel like the walls are closing in, and you are overwhelmed with

choices. Should you terminate? Should you keep the baby or adopt it out? Should you tell the father? Your parents? Where will you live and how will you deal with finances? Don't panic. God has not left you to manage on your own.

We all make mistakes. Sex outside of marriage which results in pregnancy is just more noticeable than many other sins. This book has not been written with the intention of making anyone feel guilty. It's about providing insight, information and support not only for the girl who is unexpectedly pregnant but also for her friends and family who are supporting her.

This immensely practical book looks at all the options from a Christian perspective, starting with the realization that the child in the womb is "already a life" and that this should be the place to move forward from. *A Life Already Started* also looks at how we, as God's people, can genuinely love and support women who did not intend to become pregnant.[1]

Most young women who become sexually intimate with a guy don't do so because they want to get pregnant. In reality, that consequence is often the furthest thing from their mind. When it happens and the realization hits, it's like all of the air is sucked out of the room. *How could this have happened?* Being a teenage girl is emotional enough—being a pregnant teenage girl has the potential to be emotionally explosive.

Don't panic. Pray. Ask God to help direct your path—and as much as possible, make your decisions from rational facts and not on emotional feelings. Get all the information you can, read the books I've recommended, and talk with the supportive people you trust.

A Word About Choice

I'm going to talk about something that most books for young Christian women don't discuss—abortion.

Today, the volatile pro-life versus pro-choice debate has polarized our nation. Because this topic played such an important part in my life journey to understand more about healthy boundaries and God's will, I feel an obligation to share my thoughts with you.

When I discovered I was pregnant at 15, I never considered not having my child or giving the baby up for adoption. My only thought was to escape from a brutally violent relationship and save my unborn child's life. However, after my son was born, I had two abortions, the first when I was 19, the second when I was in my midtwenties.

I've made many poor choices over the years, but *the biggest mistakes in my entire life were the two abortion choices I made.* I carried the immense weight of guilt and shame for decades.

My abortion choices took place during a time in my life when I had fully bought the lie that I deserved to have everything I wanted—that it was my right to control my body, my destiny, my life, and my future, and that no one could tell me otherwise. Clearly, it was all about *me.*

At that time, the pro-life community wasn't very strong. The pro-choice movement had center stage and was shouting the loudest. They were very convincing in their arguments, so I felt justified in my pro-choice decision. What a fool I was! No one talked about grief or any long-term effects of having an abortion. No one mentioned that my choices would come back years later to haunt me in unimaginable ways. No one told me they would leave emptiness in my soul that I would try to fill with drugs, alcohol, empty relationships, and frivolous pursuits.

> No one talked about grief or any long-term effects of having an abortion. No one mentioned that my choices would come back years later to haunt me in unimaginable ways.

Since the 1973 *Roe v. Wade* decision changed the course of our nation, people of all ages, denominations, and ethnicities are dealing with the aftereffects of choosing abortion. These aftereffects are largely undisclosed before the procedure, so that makes them even harder to process when they occur. How could we know there would be negative feelings when we believed the lie that it wasn't *a baby with a heartbeat* but simply *a choice without a consequence?*

In a survey conducted by Open Arms Ministry, 80 percent of the women who had abortions reported problems with guilt, 70 percent reported depression, 50 percent said they couldn't forgive themselves, and 76 percent said they would not have the abortion again.[2]

Look very closely at the following statistics:

- 50% of U.S. women obtaining abortions are younger than 25; women aged 20-24 obtain 33% of all U.S. abortions and teenagers obtain 17%.

- In 2009, adolescents under 15 years obtained .05% of all abortions, but had the highest abortion ratio, 785 abortions for every 1000 live births.[3]

I know firsthand there is a world of hurting women out there, trying to be daughters, sisters, wives, mothers, and friends while harboring the dark choice of abortion that keeps them in unexpected bondage. If you are (or become) pregnant, please think and pray very hard before you make the choice to join them.

Who Makes the Choice?

Some young women have aborted their babies because at the time they felt they had no choice in the matter. Perhaps a boyfriend, parent, or guardian was pressuring them, and they knew of nowhere else to go for help. I'm not suggesting that we make excuses for poor choices, but many times poor choices come out of desperate situations. Many women would have made the choice to have the baby they carried into the abortion clinic, but at the time they felt powerless to take any other steps.

You need to know that *you are not powerless—not* having an abortion is your choice to make, and you have the right to make that choice.

The Justice Foundation and the Center Against Forced Abortions have developed a formal letter that pregnant teen girls can give to their parents or anyone who may be forcefully encouraging them to abort against their will. Simply put, parents cannot pressure their daughter into an abortion. You can download that letter from this website:

thejusticefoundation.org/wp-content/uploads/2011/05/
Dear-Parent-Oct2010.pdf

In essence, this is what the letter says about your rights:

"It violates even her constitutional right to make the decision to have an abortion," explains attorney Allan Parker, who heads the legal group. "And even though we're a parents' rights organization, people need to remember that when a girl is pregnant, she's now a mother. She has parental rights."

According to Parker, most parents and underage girls don't know that the girl can refuse to kill her preborn child. The letter to parents states (in part):

"As a mother, she has the fundamental right to direct the upbringing and education of her child. That right is hers—not anyone else's…Any third party (including a relative) who causes the baby to be killed may be guilty of fetal homicide."

In addition, parents cannot make threats of violence or apply excessive coercion to force an abortion. A method frequently used to force a girl to have an abortion—i.e., threatening to throw her out of the house if she refuses—not only terrifies the child, says the attorney, but is also illegal.[4]

A Very Painful Choice

Every woman considering abortion needs to understand the long-term effects of this choice. After an abortion, many women attempt to bury their grief, turn their emotions off, and run from God. Eventually they face the fact that abortion ended their unborn baby's life.

Abortion did not end my pain. In fact, it was the catalyst for the pain and dysfunction that robbed me for so long of happiness and love. My pain, guilt, and destructive behavior hurt not only me but also all those around me during the years I tried to bury my guilt and shame.

The late pastor Lowell Lundstrom once said an amazing thing during a media interview. "I believe in pro-choice!" he exclaimed to the surprise of the reporter. "Sure I do. I believe every woman can choose to have sex or not. But if she becomes pregnant as a result of that choice, then it becomes a baby—not a choice—and it's out of her hands."

Today, I agree with that sentiment. In my opinion, there are only two choices available when you are pregnant—to raise the baby as your own or to place the child for adoption.

The Adoption Choice

Now there's a choice that was never presented to me at the abortion clinics—adoption. Why didn't I consider the countless parents who couldn't conceive and who were aching to have a child? Because that would mean carrying the baby full term, allowing the world to see what I had done, and then dealing with the aftereffects of placing the baby for adoption. Back then it simply wasn't done. Today, choosing adoption can be one of the most loving and responsible choices a pregnant young woman can make.

Being a mother is life changing—not just for you but also for your child. Your ability to be emotionally, psychologically, and spiritually whole and healthy are paramount in raising a child.

It's a huge responsibility. Make certain you are ready for it.

If you find that you are not—please know there are many people who long to be parents but cannot. God has someone who is ready, willing, able, and anxiously waiting to wrap their arms and heart around your baby.

The Motherhood Choice

If you make the choice to raise your baby and be a mom, there's an amazing resource I'd like to share with you. It's a book by Tricia Goyer called *Life Interrupted: The Scoop on Being a Young Mom*.

Without a doubt, this is a must-have resource for every teen mom. Tricia was 15 when she got pregnant the first time and made a choice that she lived to regret. She was 17 when she got pregnant again and decided to make a different choice.

> Becoming a mother has helped some young moms stop to consider what they want from life. It's helped them get on track.
>
> Before I got pregnant, I didn't think much about my future.

When I was in elementary school, I used to dream about life as an adult, but when high school rolled around, "future thinking" took a back seat to "having fun today." What mattered most was who was playing in the football game Friday night, where the party was Saturday night, and what could I do so my hangover wouldn't give me away on Sunday morning.

Once I became pregnant, though, I realized that my plans for a good future were not only vital for me, they were also important for my child. My thought process changed. I now wondered, What should I do about schooling? What classes can I take at the community college to help me in a future career? What job would I enjoy that will still allow me to spend quality time with my son?

Right now, your major decisions may center on your schooling options. Or they may concern where you should work or live. No matter what choices you're facing, mothering provides an opportunity to become a better person. A better person for yourself. For your future. For your child.[5]

Today, Tricia Goyer is a busy mom of six, grandmother of two, and wife to John. A bestselling author, Tricia has published 37 books to date and has written more than 500 articles. (She also wrote the foreword to this book.)

In 2010, SheKnows.com selected Tricia as one of the Top 20 Moms to Follow on Twitter. Tricia is also on the blogging team at MomLifeToday.com, TheBetterMom.com, and other homeschooling and Christian sites. In addition to her roles as mom, wife, and author, Tricia volunteers around her community and mentors teen moms. She is the founder of Hope Pregnancy Ministries in northwestern Montana, and she currently leads a teen Mothers of Preschoolers (MOPS) group in Little Rock, Arkansas. She also hosts the weekly radio podcast *Living Inspired*. You can learn more about Tricia at www.triciagoyer.com.

In addition to words and insight from *Life Interrupted*, Tricia has graciously allowed me to share a post from her *Living Inspired* blog. Tricia wrote it for adults who are in a position to influence and support pregnant teens, and I encourage you to share it with the influential adults in your life. I hope Tricia's words and insight will bless and inspire you.

I'm Here to Blow Your Teen Pregnancy Statistics Out of the Water

I had my first baby when I was seventeen. It was hard, but I can't imagine how a young mom who's living in New York City feels these days. Have you seen the posters plastered all over the subways in the media? One shows a crying baby and reads, "I'm twice as likely not to graduate from high school because you had me as a teen."

While it's true that having a baby as a teen is hard, choosing to have the baby IS a good decision. It's a selfless, caring decision that will give the child a future, planned or not.

Instead of trying to shame a teen mom, what if you, me, we…supported her? Would her child still be a sad statistic if there was a group of men and women who educated her, inspired her, and offered her hope?

That's what happened to me. A group of older woman came alongside me. They taught me about being a mom. They made me feel as if I had value. They saw my child as a gift. They painted a bright future. Because of them, my confidence as a mom grew. My confidence as a woman grew. I married, and I birthed two more children. Where are those kids now? My oldest son is a college graduate with a great job, a wife, and a child. My daughter will be graduating with her bachelor's degree at age twenty and is moving to Europe for a year to teach English. My eighteen-year-old son is a college freshman (getting straight A's I might add). Not only that, my husband and I have adopted three little ones! I also mentor teen mothers, just as those women mentored me.

I could have been a statistic, but instead a group of women offered to impart hope into my heart. Now I impart hope into others, not only through mentoring, but also through books.

I'm forty-one years old, and I have thirty-seven published books from publishers such as HarperCollins and Random House. I impart hope through parenting books and even through my novels. In fact my new release is an Amish novel, *The Promise Box*, about a young Amish woman trying to discover herself— and the reason for her life—after she finds out she was conceived by a rape. She learns she is [valuable] and will never be just a statistic.

Maybe today...or tomorrow...you might have a young woman come to you for advice after she discovers she's pregnant. Don't point her to a NYC subway sign. Instead, here's a few ways you can help:

Remain calm and loving. Your young friend most likely feels alone, frightened, and extremely sensitive about her pregnancy. The most important thing you can offer is your continued friendship.

Show God's love and forgiveness. Your young friend was looking for love by giving herself intimately to a guy. Now she might feel ashamed and unworthy of love at all. Point her to God, who loves her unconditionally.

Celebrate life. She may consider this baby a "mistake"—a barrier between her and "normal" life. Lovingly remind her that no matter how the baby was conceived, he or she is a gift from God.

Be available to share...and to listen. Your young friend has many big decisions to make, and although you can't make those decisions for her, you can be available to help her consider her options. Share information you've discovered on fetal development and on the physical and emotional trauma of abortion. Most of all, be willing to listen to her deepest concerns.

Find help. Your young friend is most likely in need of more answers than you can give. Visit a local crisis pregnancy center with your friend, or call CareNet for help at 1-800-395-HELP.

Encourage her to tell her parents and to seek the counsel of a pastor or youth pastor.

Yes, the young woman and her baby will face a hard road ahead. But with your help, encouragement, and gift of hope you can help her to also blow the teen pregnancy statistics out of the water.[6]

A Final Word

Cindy was an only child, but her mother always longed to have a big family. Sadly, that wasn't God's plan for her life. When Cindy discovered she was pregnant, her mother saw it as her own second chance at motherhood.

> When I got pregnant in my senior year of high school, my boyfriend and I knew we weren't ready to be parents, and we decided together to place our baby for adoption. However, my mother saw this as her opportunity to raise another baby, and she was adamant in voicing her outrage over our choice. She did everything in her power to convince—and force me to keep the baby, including bribery, threats, guilt, and shame. She wasn't thinking about what was best for the child—she was focused on what she thought was best for her. When I needed her support and love the most, all I got was anger and resentment. Our relationship has never been the same, but I know in my heart that adoption was the best choice.

Be aware that you have rights—even as a teen—and speak up if you are facing someone's use of excessive control or force concerning your pregnancy, whether it's to keep, adopt, or abort your child.

And remember, with all rights comes responsibility, and there is no greater responsibility than raising a child.

Through it all, continue to apply the "A" step and *Assemble Supportive People*. Pray to God and ask for the Spirit of truth to guide you.

17

Accept Responsibility— Develop Your Plan of Action

Young Adults naturally tend to act impulsively and emotionally on occasion. After all, you're on the road to maturity—you haven't arrived there yet. However, just because you're young doesn't mean you automatically get a pass to make poor choices and behave irresponsibly without consequences. The fact is, you have the ability to play an active part in your journey to become a confident, capable, and responsible adult.

For example, if you know you have trouble setting boundaries in a specific situation, and if you wait until you're in that situation again before deciding how you're going to respond rationally, you'll almost certainly default to your old behavior. In other words, you'll find yourself back on the gerbil wheel of insanity—repeating the same behavior and expecting different results. "This time will be different," you'll say...but will it really?

> You can accept the responsibility now for making your life better— for becoming the best *you* possible.

The way to make sure the outcome is different is to train yourself to change now—if indeed you want to—before the next situation arises. You can accept the responsibility now for making your life better—for becoming the best *you* possible.

When you apply the "S" step in SANITY, you are making the intentional decision to *Stop* doing (or accepting) something negative that is contributing to your stress. You are reprogramming yourself to *Stop* ignoring your pain and problems and face them head on. You are training your brain to *respond rationally* and not *react emotionally*, and to consider the consequences of your actions *before* acting. Applying this step is an excellent way to build strong character. Mastering this technique will help you become competent in many areas of life.

Remember, self-worth comes from character, competence, and smart choices. One of the smartest choices you can make as a teen is to develop a written plan of action that identifies the areas where you'd like to see yourself grow or change.

Nothing can move forward and still remain the same. Change is necessary for progress. And you can make the choice to change most anything you want to change. You can learn new things. You can set a new course. You can decide today to *Stop* ignoring your pain and problems. You can cope with the overwhelming stress in your life and find sanity in all of your choices. Having a written plan of action can help you resist negative peer pressure, drugs, sexual temptation, emotional entanglements with the wrong kind of males, and other potentially harmful influences. More importantly, it can help you strategically guide your life to achieve success in whatever endeavor or field you choose. And it does this by causing you to intentionally think—and write—about who you are and what you want.

> By learning and memorizing the SANITY Steps, Christy was able to break the habit of reacting emotionally when her friend challenged her to shoplift.

When you have a plan and you are faced with a tough decision, you can ask yourself, "Does this fit with who I am and who I want to be? What did I write in my plan of action about this situation?"

Remember Christy? She knew she had a tendency to say yes to things that were wrong because she was afraid of not fitting in—of being ostracized by her peers. However, now she was tired of being ruled by her fears. She realized she had to *Stop* being someone she wasn't. She needed to consider whether her responses and actions would help her reach her goals and fulfill her plans—not whether they would help her fit in.

By learning and memorizing the SANITY Steps, Christy was able to break the habit of reacting emotionally when her friend challenged her to shoplift. If she accepted the challenge and got caught, one of the consequences to breaking the law was going to jail, and Christy didn't think that risk was worth the fear of not fitting in.

Smart girl.

The Gift of Self-Discipline

When we hear the word "discipline," we think of punishment. But it can also refer to training or instruction. As children and then as teenagers, we don't always grasp that what we learn as young people will establish who we become as adults. That's why the training and instruction we receive during this stage of life is so important.

It's good to have someone in your corner who believes in you, someone who extends discipline with love and respect, sees your potential, and encourages you to push yourself to the next level. However, your personal success isn't dependent on whether you have a cheerleader. It begins as you...

- make the choice—perhaps despite your feelings—to believe in yourself
- understand who you are and envision who you want to become
- accept responsibility for your thoughts, behaviors, attitudes, and actions

When you see a concert pianist, an amazing dancer, an Olympic athlete, a gifted singer, or an amazing artist, you're seeing someone who invested countless hours of training and instruction into perfecting their craft. The same goes for scientists, doctors, lawyers, teachers, and countless business and trade professionals.

> Self-discipline is an amazing and powerful gift you can give yourself.

When you want something with all of your heart and soul, when you feel led to pursue a specific area of expertise or to make specific changes in your life, the required self-discipline is much easier to take. When we have a reason to be self-disciplined, our perspective of the world changes. Self-discipline is an amazing and powerful gift you can give yourself.

However, not everyone knows what they want to do with their future, and that is perfectly understandable and acceptable. If you're in this situation, don't be hard on yourself—discovering your purpose in life is part of the growing-up process. If you don't yet know what you want for the future, start by getting real about who you are now. Believe in yourself, work hard, and be willing to accept responsibility for your thoughts, behavior, attitudes, values, character, identity, and future.

Eventually, when you discover your calling, you'll be ready to do what it takes to follow the call and achieve your dream.

Get Ready, Get Set, and Go!

You are never more vulnerable or more invincible than when you are a teen. You can do anything! Conversely, sometimes you feel as if you can't do anything right. You're a mess of jumbled emotions, yet the fact remains—you have infinite possibilities!

There's a saying that if you aim for nothing, you'll hit it every time. If you don't have a written map to chart your course, you're likely to get lost at some point on the journey—especially if the weather turns bad or the terrain gets rocky. That's why the "I" Step in SANITY is an important part at any stage of life. Take the time very soon to *Implement Your Plan of Action* by writing down your answers to the questions listed under "7 Directions to Help Chart Your Life Course" (page 174). Then choose one special date to revise this plan every year. For example, you could make this a part of every New Year, birthday, or other special date that is significant to you. Make sure to put the date at the top of every plan, and keep all of them in a file on your computer or in a keepsake box. You'll want to look back on these plans over the years to see your success and to thank God for the ways He answered your prayers—sometimes with a yes and sometimes with a no. Trusting God with your life is the major part of becoming who He wants you to be—and who *you* want to be.

When you sit down to revise your plan of action every year, focus on yearly goals. Otherwise the annual exercise might seem overwhelming. For example, I've taken the liberty to establish a key focus for your first plan of action—"Set Healthy Boundaries and Cope with Stress." Keep that focus in mind as you develop your written plan.

Give yourself time to develop this plan. Don't rush it. Be thoughtful and thorough—you're worth it!

Remember, anything that is alive and vibrant is always growing and changing. When something is dead, it ceases to grow or change. Aspiring to embrace change will help develop your character and competence and will increase your self-worth as you take a proactive role in becoming the person God wants you to be.

A Critical Aspect of a Successful Plan of Action

As part of your ongoing success in applying the "I" step—*Implement a Plan of Action*—allocate yourself a quiet time of reflection every day to seek God's will, pray, listen, and to apply the "T" step in SANITY—*Trust the Voice of the Spirit.*

After you complete your first written plan of action, I challenge you to read your Bible, pray, and continue to write your thoughts in a journal every day. Strive to make the daily habit of spiritual reflection second nature.

Start your day with the true breakfast of champions—a Word from God from the Bible and a prayer to God. Spending time with God every day is a spiritual discipline that will change your life. As you pray, ask God to reveal His will to you. Learning to recognize God's voice may take time, but you can trust that your heavenly Father is always listening and always working in your life.

Remember that you cannot control God and His plans for your life. The fact is, He may have something entirely different planned for you. Trust that He is directing the action behind the scenes—even allowing Satan to pull your strings, sometimes to the breaking point. Just trust and believe that through it all, God knows what He is doing.

> Teach me your decrees, O Lord;
> I will keep them to the end.

Give me understanding and I will obey your instructions;
   I will put them into practice with all my heart.
Make me walk along the path of your commands,
   for that is where my happiness is found
   (Psalm 119:33-35 NLT).

7 Directions to Help Chart Your Life Course

1. Be proactive and take responsibility for your life.
2. Set your standards and define your identity.
3. Balance your slice-of-life pie.
4. Identify your goals and dreams.
5. Establish the actions needed to change your negative thoughts, behaviors, and attitudes.
6. Consider the consequences of making changes.
7. Envision the rewards on your journey of change.

Name: _____

Date: _____

Location (City/State): _____

Action Plan 1
This Year's Focus: Set Healthy Boundaries and Cope with Stress

1. Be proactive and take responsibility for your life.

- What does taking responsibility for your life mean to you right now?
- What has God revealed to your heart about past actions that may have been irresponsible?
- What is the relationship between taking responsibility and coping with stress?
- List the negative thoughts, behaviors, and attitudes you want to stop.

2. Set your standards and define your identity.

- What do values, integrity, and character mean to you?
- Who and what defines your identity?
- Take time to develop these three lists: your top-ten values, your top-ten character traits, and the top-ten signs that you have integrity.

3. Balance your slice-of-life pie.

- What does placing God at the center of your life mean to you?
- List all six slices of life and ask God to reveal what He wants you to know about each area. Does He want you to change anything in any of the slices? If so, what? Write down your thoughts and spiritual revelation under each area.
- Which areas are your strongest? Your weakest?

4. Identify your goals and dreams.

- What do you want to be when you grow up?
- Why do you think this is your calling?
- If you are uncertain of your calling, what areas interest you and why?
- What do you most often dream about?

5. Establish the actions needed to change negative thoughts, behaviors, and attitudes.

- Refer to the list of things you want to change (in number 1 above) and prioritize them here, beginning with the most important.
- Write down the actions you need to begin to implement change in each item. For example, if you want to treat your

sister with more respect, one of your actions may be to ask her permission before you wear any of her clothing. Another action could be that you stop calling her names and stop making fun of her curly hair.

- Once you decide to make specific changes, some actions you need to take will be very clear, but others may be murky and harder to establish. Consider asking for advice regarding possible actions you can take in the situations you've listed.

6. Consider the consequences of making changes.

Do your best to calculate the risks involved when you begin to take action and make changes, and write down every possible consequence you can think of that may happen when you begin to respond differently to this person or in this situation. What roadblocks might you encounter?

For example, when Christy developed her plan, one of her priority issues was to stop saying yes to the mean but popular girl in her clique—something she did because she was afraid of not fitting in. She worked with her counselor to brainstorm every potential consequence, which included the possibility of being ostracized, bullied at school, attacked in social networking sites, threatened, physically assaulted, and so on. In reality, the fallout from saying no wasn't as bad as she thought it might be, but she was prepared for just about anything.

Example 1

- *Negative behavior to change*—Stop being afraid of not fitting in and sacrificing my standards and integrity.
- *Action to take*—Say no in a firm yet kind way when I feel my boundaries are being violated (don't be angry or emotional).
- *Consequences*—The popular girls might ignore me, I might not have anyone to hang out with on the weekends, I might be the subject of a social networking smear campaign, and so on.

Example 2

- *Negative behavior to change*—Stop being rude and disrespectful to my sister.
- *Action to take*—Ask her permission before borrowing clothing.
- *Consequences*—We will fight less and things might be more peaceful around the house. Mom will appreciate this. I will stop feeling guilty for hurting my sister's feelings.

7. Envision the rewards on your journey of change.

- Make a list of the rewards for placing God at the center of your life.
- Make a list of the rewards for setting healthy boundaries.
- Make a list of the rewards for having biblical standards and acting with integrity.
- Make a list of the rewards for using the SANITY Steps to cope with your current stress.

A Final Word About Responsibility and Action

Congratulations for making it this far in your journey of self-discovery!

We've discussed a lot of heavy issues. Your personal exploration may have been uncomfortable sometimes—even painful. But it's only in the examination of life that we spread our wings and stretch ourselves to become all that we can be—all that God wants us to be.

I am so proud of you.

Far more important, your heavenly Father is proud of you.

> It's only in the examination of life that we spread our wings and stretch ourselves to become all that we can be—all that God wants us to be.

18

How to Assemble a
SANITY Support Group

Having a group of like-minded peers who can read this book together and form their own SANITY Support Group can be a very powerful thing. No matter where you are on your own journey to set healthy boundaries and find sanity, you can be the person God uses to facilitate a group learning process through weekly reading, studying, and sharing. The Holy Spirit will be the Teacher, but you can be the instrument through whom God does His work.

A SANITY Support Group is a safe place to meet and confidentially discuss boundary topics from this book. It's where you can talk openly about how to cope with stress, break bad habits, and develop healthy boundaries by applying the Six Steps to SANITY. A SANITY Support Group is a great place to develop your written plan of action and to share strategies for implementing your plan and making smart choices. It's a place where responsibility and accountability reign, the power of prayer rocks, and God's Word rules.

It's important to have fun and build relationships of trust and acceptance, but a SANITY Support Group is not a glorified gossip session. It's not a place to talk about boys or other girls. It's not an environment of judgment or condemnation. And it's not a place where excuses thrive or consequences hide.

In reality, participating in a SANITY Support Group can be a life-changing and empowering experience for young women who are ready to let God help them learn how to make choices that will change their lives.

You can find more details about how to start and facilitate a SANITY Support Group of your own by visiting our website and clicking on the appropriate page under the SANITY Support menu bar. By taking part in candid discussions on our Facebook page, you can also discover how other young women are coordinating SANITY Support groups around the country.

In the meantime, I encourage you to pray about starting your own group. Grab your journal and write down ways that God is impressing this desire on your heart. Ask Him to give you wisdom and discernment, to open doors to make it happen, and to bring you like-minded friends who are ready and willing to stop the insanity of stress and embrace the hope and healing that come from learning how to set healthy boundaries.

If you feel led to accept this responsibility, you can trust God to equip and enable you to accomplish the task. You can trust that God is in control and that He has a divine plan and purpose for bringing you to this special place of coordinating a peer support group.

Visit our website:
SettingBoundariesBooks.com

Visit our Facebook community:
Facebook.com/SanitySupportforYoungWomen

Share this book with friends and
encourage them to find sanity with you.

19

In Closing

Here's the bottom line. None of us can fulfill God's purpose for our life if we don't take setting healthy boundaries seriously. Boundaries are good for us because God doesn't want us to live in bondage to the pain, expectations, worry, fear, depression, and stress that come with a life of no boundaries.

That is not the life He has planned for you or for me.

You are on God's mission, with His authority, power, love, grace, and mercy—everything you need to make smart choices at any stage in your life. God wants you to have a new understanding of Him, of the Bible, and of your identity in Christ.

It takes faith and courage to stand up and do what is right in tough situations and circumstances. In the Bible we read of David, who had faith he could kill the giant Goliath. Still, it took courage for him to walk into that arena with nothing but a slingshot to take out Goliath. David's faith rested in knowing that the Lord was with him and that God would provide everything he needed to slay the enemy. And his courage came from his willingness to confront fear, pain, danger, uncertainty, and intimidation.

But David had a secret. He knew whose side he was on—and who was on his side.

Like David, you too can hold tight to your faith and trust the Lord to be on your side. Ask God to strengthen your character, integrity, and standards, and to give you the courage to rise above your pain and problems and put an end to the stranglehold of stress in your life.

> If you stand for nothing, you'll fall for everything.

You can change your life as you follow God's standards and apply the Six Steps to SANITY to the troubling situations and circumstances that will inevitably come your way. Know this important fact—if you stand for nothing, you'll fall for everything.

Also know that you can be a mighty influence in the lives of your peers—other young women who are searching for their identity, who are struggling with the overwhelming burden of stress, and who want desperately to find meaning and purpose in their lives.

Let God use you to be an instrument of love, forgiveness, and peace.

And always remember, you are never without a pilot—even when you don't know which way to steer.

God's Word

The Bible is filled with words of wisdom, and I pray that you will grow to depend on it not only in times of trouble and confusion, but throughout all of your life. However, one particular book of the Bible is devoted solely to imparting nuggets of wisdom, advice, and guidance that can be a source of strength on your journey as a twenty-first-century teen. I'd like to end our time together by sharing some verses from the first chapter of this book, and I encourage you to study this important and empowering chapter.

May the God of love and peace always be with you.

Allison

PS: Please stay in touch! Stop by my Facebook author page to join our growing community of readers and to let me know how setting boundaries and finding SANITY has changed your life.

Facebook.com/AuthorAllisonBottke

And be sure to check out our special SANITY Support for Young Women community on Facebook as well. Soak up the inspiration, share your thoughts, and find sanity on your journey to make smart choices and set healthy boundaries!

Facebook.com/SanitySupportforYoungWomen

The Purpose of Proverbs

These are the proverbs of Solomon, David's son, king of Israel.

Their purpose is to teach people wisdom and discipline,
    to help them understand the insights of the wise.
Their purpose is to teach people to live disciplined and successful
    lives, to help them do what is right, just, and fair.
These proverbs will give insight to the simple,
    knowledge and discernment to the young.

Let the wise listen to these proverbs and become even wiser.
    Let those with understanding receive guidance
by exploring the meaning in these proverbs and parables,
    the words of the wise and their riddles.

Fear of the LORD is the foundation of true knowledge,
    but fools despise wisdom and discipline
    (Proverbs 1:1-7 NLT).

Notes

Chapter 2: The Scoop on Boundaries

1. Henry Cloud and John Townsend, *Boundaries: When to Say Yes, How to Say No to Take Control of Your Life* (Grand Rapids, MI: Zondervan, 1992), 73.

2. Cloud and Townsend, *Boundaries*, 73.

Chapter 3: It's All in Your Mind

1. Allison Bottke, *God Allows U-Turns for Teens: The Choices We Make Change the Story of Our Life* (Minneapolis, MN: Bethany House, 2006), 21-23.

Chapter 4: Just Say No to Stress and Yes to Love

1. "Just Say No," Wikipedia, en.wikipedia.org/wiki/Just_Say_No.

Chapter 5: The Center of Balance

1. Debra D. Peppers, *It's Your Turn Now!* (Kirkwood, MO: Impact Christian Books, 2001), 84.

Chapter 6: The Foundation of Faith

1. Michelle McKinney Hammond and Joel A. Brooks Jr., *The Unspoken Rules of Love* (Colorado Springs, CO: Waterbrook Press, 2003), 30.

2. Sean Covey, *The 6 Most Important Decisions You'll Ever Make* (New York, NY: Fireside, 2006), 280.

Chapter 8: Claim Your Identity—Understand Your Value

1. Allison Bottke, *God Allows U-Turns for Teens: The Choices We Make Change the Story of Our Life* (Minneapolis, MN: Bethany House, 2006), 85-88.

2. June Hunt, *Seeing Yourself Through God's Eyes* (Eugene, OR: Harvest House, 2008), 10.

3. Rebecca Musser, *The Witness Wore Red* (New York, NY: Grand Central, 2013), 332.

4. June Hunt, *Counseling Through Your Bible Handbook: Providing Biblical Hope and Practical Help for 50 Everyday Problems* (Eugene, OR: Harvest House, 2008), 237-38.

5. Hunt, *Counseling Through Your Bible Handbook*, 240.

Chapter 9: Unpack Your Emotional Baggage

1. John Stossel, quoting Suffolk University professor Jane Bybee, "Is Guilt Good for You?" ABC News, January 17, 2013, abcnews.go.com/2020/story?id=123763&page=1.

Chapter 11: Under the Dome of Pressure

1. "Suicide Prevention: Youth Suicide," The Centers for Disease Control and Prevention, www.cdc.gov/violenceprevention/pub/youth_suicide.html.

Chapter 12: The Exhaustion of Expectations

1. Joyce Meyer, *Teenagers Are People Too!* (New York, NY: Warner Faith, 2002), 13-14.

Chapter 13: Violated Boundaries

1. "Senator Mike Crapo says no more: 'We have a responsibility to help nurture healthy relationships and reduce domestic violence,'" The NO MORE Project, July 29, 2013, nomore.org/senator-mike-crapo-says-no-more-we-have-a-responsibility-to-help-nurture-healthy-relationships-and-reduce-domestic-violence/.

2. Liz Brody, "Relationship Violence: The Secret That Kills 4 Women a Day," *Glamour*, June 2011, www.glamour.com/tell-somebody/2011/05/relationship-violence-the-secret-that-kills-4-women-a-day.

3. "Child Sex Trafficking," National Center for Missing and Exploited Children, www.missingkids.com/CSTT.

4. "Innocence Lost," The US Department of Justice Federal Bureau of Investigation, www.fbi.gov/about-us/investigate/vc_majorthefts/cac/innocencelost.

5. Mary DeMuth, *The Wall Around Your Heart: How Jesus Heals You When Others Hurt You* (Nashville, TN: Thomas Nelson, 2013), 6-7.

Chapter 14: Internet Predators and Cyberbullies

1. "A Parent's Guide to Internet Safety," the US Department of Justice Federal Bureau of Investigation, www.fbi.gov/stats-services/publications/parent-guide.

2. "Why Has Cyberbullying Become a Major Issue?" End to Cyber Bullying, www.endcyberbullying.org/why-has-cyberbullying-become-a-major-issue/.

3. "11 Facts About Cyber Bullying," DoSomething.org, www.dosomething.org/tipsandtools/11-facts-about-cyber-bullying.

Chapter 15: Teen Dating Violence

1. "Teen Dating Violence," Centers for Disease Control and Prevention, www.cdc.gov/violenceprevention/intimatepartnerviolence/teen_dating_violence.html.

2. Diane Lefer, "Teen Dating Violence—a V-Day Panel," *Nobody Wakes Up Pretty* (blog), February 16, 2013, dianelefer.wordpress.com/tag/barrie-levy/. Lefer is citing Barrie Levy's comments to the Los Angeles chapter of the National Council of Jewish Women on February 14, 2013.

3. Barrie Levy, *In Love and in Danger: A Teen's Guide to Breaking Free of Abusive Relationships* (Seattle, WA: Seal Press, 1993), 52-53.

4. Levy, *In Love and in Danger*, 53.

Chapter 16: Life Interrupted—a Baby Changes Everything

1. "A life already started," Fervr, fervr.net/a-life-already-started.

2. "Open Arms Reports Survey Results," *Ludington Daily News*, November 3, 1994, news.google.com/newspapers?nid=110&dat=19941103&id=cEZQAAAAIBAJ&sjid=rVUDAAAAIBAJ&pg=7331,3151226.

3. "U.S. Abortion Statistics," Abort73.com, Loxafamosity Ministries, June 21, 2013, www.abort73.com/abortion_facts/us_abortion_statistics/.

4. Charlie Butts, "Pregnant teens can't be forced to have abortions—by anyone," OneNews Now.com, Friday, August 09, 2013, www.onenewsnow.com/legal-courts/2013/08/09/pregnant-teens-can%E2%80%99t-be-forced-to-have-abortions-%E2%80%93-by-anyone#.UpJX18Si3Ak.

5. Tricia Goyer, *Life Interrupted: The Scoop on Being a Young Mom* (Grand Rapids, MI: Zondervan, 2004), 32-33.

6. Tricia Goyer, *I'm Here to Blow Your Teen Pregnancy Statistics Out of the Water*, April 17, 2013, www.triciagoyer.com/teen-pregnancy-statistics/.

High Praise for Allison Bottke's Setting Boundaries® books...

Setting Boundaries® for Women

"I'm giving copies of this book to my girlfriends, mom, adult daughters, and the many women I care about in my life because I know this is a resource that can help us rise above our circumstances and live a more abundant life."

Ellie Kay
America's Family Financial Expert® and bestselling author

"Had I understood the content and action plans of *Setting Boundaries for Women* in my earlier years, my life would have been healthier and happier... Keep this book handy—it's a vital resource to help you throughout your life."

Jennifer Strickland
speaker and author of *Beautiful Lies* and *Girl Perfect*

"*Setting Boundaries for Women* lays out an easy-to-follow guide to help navigate difficult and challenging relationships and events that are common to us all. Allison is an accomplished author, an inspirational voice, and a role model to real people, in a real world, with real challenges. Her words will bring hope, light, and peace to multitudes of lives!"

Pastor Tiz Huch
DFW New Beginnings Church, Dallas, TX

"I was forty years old before I learned there are such things as boundaries—much less that I could enforce them in my life as a daughter, wife, mom, and friend! If only I had Allison's book *Setting Boundaries for Women* back then. Fortunate is the woman who reads this book now and puts the author's empowering principles into action...Pick up a copy for yourself and for a friend."

Karen O'Connor
author of *When God Answers Your Prayers:
How God Comes Through in the Nick of Time*

"In *Setting Boundaries for Women*, Allison reveals how boundaries are not only healthy, but the fruit of a godly life. Allison helps us to identify the areas of our life that seem out of control, and gives simple, practical steps to implement healthy boundaries from a godly perspective, with real-life examples."

Dana Pollard
songwriter and recording artist

Setting Boundaries® with Food

"Many folks who have had difficult upbringings turn to something to fill them all the way up, such as food, sex, admiration, or success. Allison peels away the layers of why we reach for that piece of chocolate cake and why it seems to have power over us. And then she adeptly points us to the One who can fill us all the way up—Jesus."

Mary DeMuth
author of *Thin Places*

Setting Boundaries® with Difficult People

"Well organized, powerfully written, thoughtful, challenging, and helpful for everyday living, this excellent volume is a keeper—a reference you'll refer to repeatedly as you encounter those inevitable aggravating relationships. Get it. Read it. Use it! And celebrate your less-stressful life."

Mary Hollingsworth
author and managing director, Creative Enterprises Studio

Setting Boundaries® with Your Aging Parents

"This book is written in the same spirit of hope, generosity, and faith that allowed the readers of Allison's first book in the Setting Boundaries series to find a sane and safe place of recovery, optimism, and healing. It is an inspiring and important addition to the body of literature that addresses the problem and pain of adult children dealing with difficult parents. It is stunningly integrated with the importance of understanding that God is the ultimate authority, overriding both societal and psychological beliefs."

Mark Sichel
LCSW and author of *Healing from Family Rifts*

Setting Boundaries® with Your Adult Children

"This book will launch a brand-new beginning in your life. You may feel you are in a desert place as you struggle with a parenting crisis, but be alert! There's a stream in the wasteland—and you can begin making hope-filled choices that will forever change your future for the better."

Carol Kent
speaker and author of *When I Lay My Isaac Down* and
A New Kind of Normal

"No one knows better the pain of dealing with adult children who have lost their way than the parents of those without boundaries. Allison Bottke, writing through her own hurt and experience, has compiled a masterpiece of advice. She doesn't just tell you or show you how it's done. She walks along beside you."

Eva Marie Everson and Jessica Everson
authors of *Sex, Lies, and the Media*

About Allison Bottke

Allison Bottke is the award-winning author of the popular Setting Boundaries series (more than 200,000 sold), which includes *Setting Boundaries with Your Adult Children*, *Setting Boundaries with Your Aging Parents*, *Setting Boundaries with Difficult People*, *Setting Boundaries with Food*, and *Setting Boundaries for Women*. She is the founder of the SANITY Support Group, an outreach based on the Setting Boundaries series. Her other books include the God Answers Prayers series, and she is the founder and general editor of over a dozen volumes in the popular God Allows U-Turns anthology. She has written or edited more than 30 nonfiction and fiction books and is a frequent guest on national radio and TV programs around the country. Allison lives in the Dallas–Fort Worth area.

You can reach her at:
SettingBoundariesBooks.com
Facebook.com/AuthorAllisonBottke

To learn more about Harvest House books
or to read sample chapters, visit our website:

HarvestHousePublishers.com

HARVEST HOUSE PUBLISHERS
EUGENE, OREGON